Claudia Perren and Sarah Breen Lovett, Editors
Expanded Architecture —
Temporal Spatial Practices

Bauhaus Edition 47

1.1

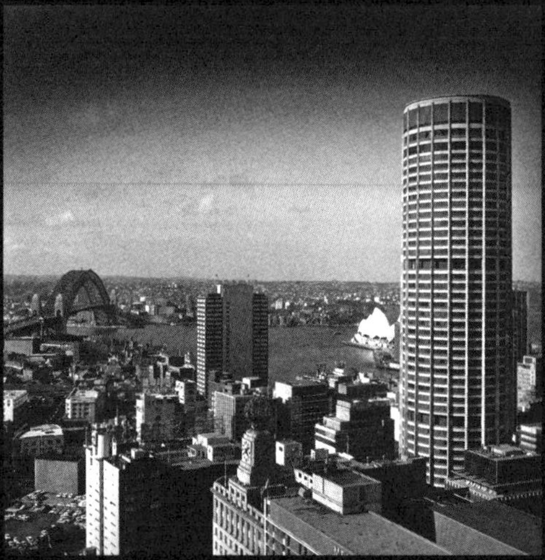

1.2

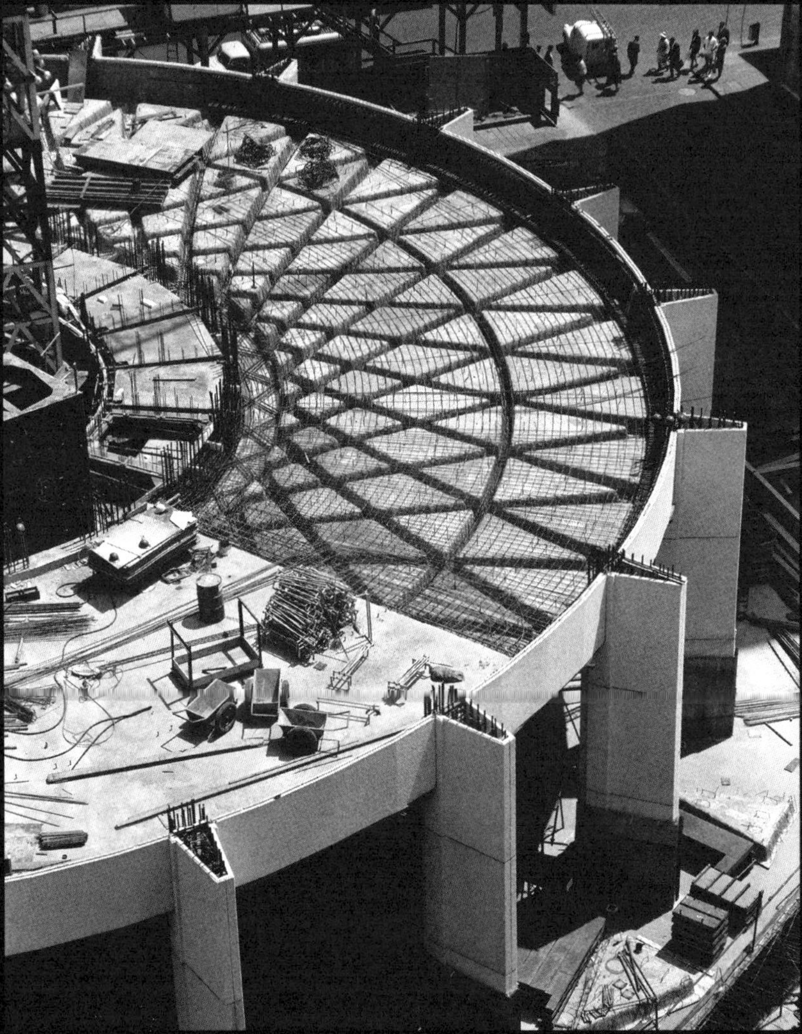

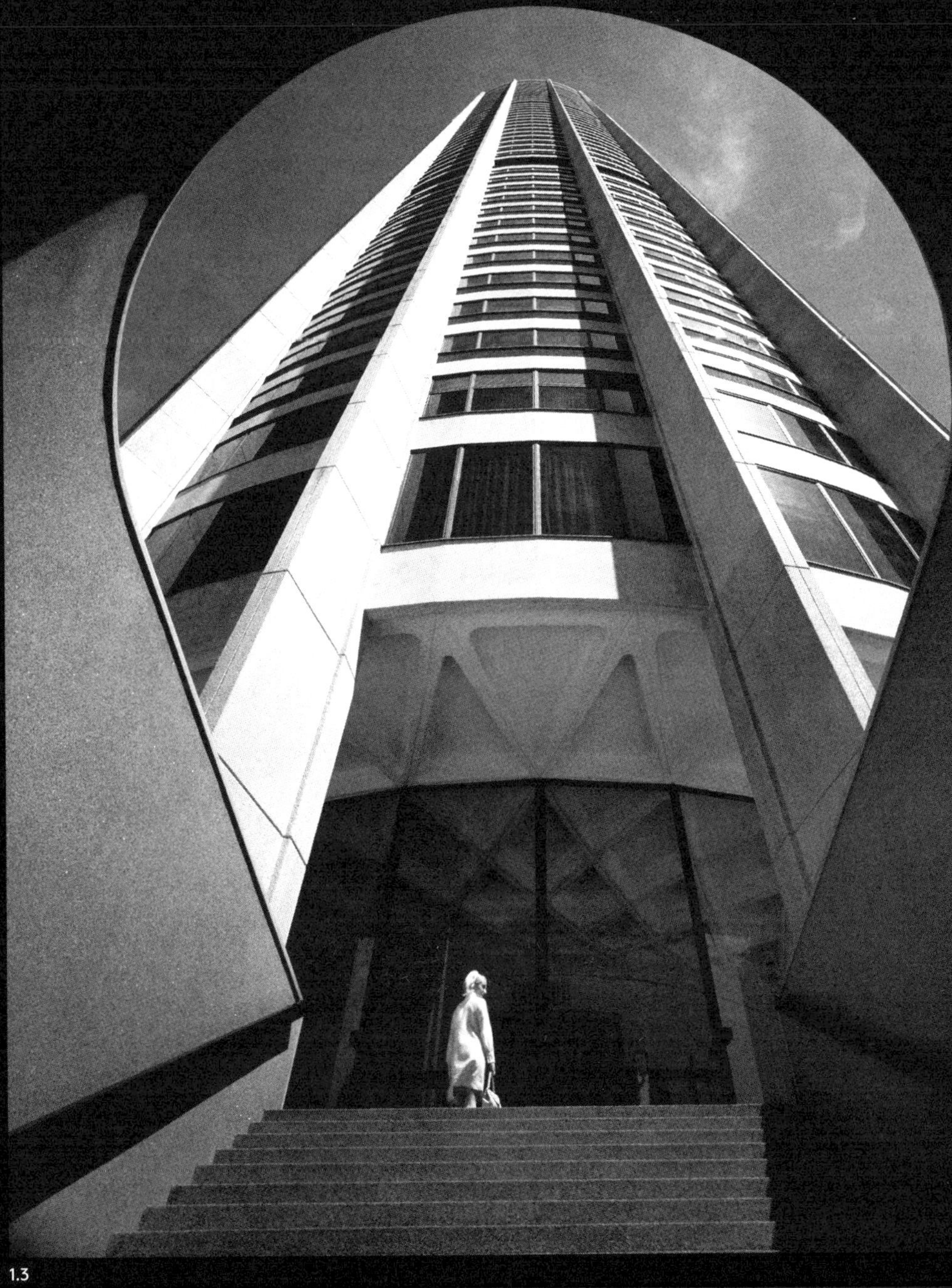

1.3

Australia Square, 1961–67.

E

X

P A

2.1

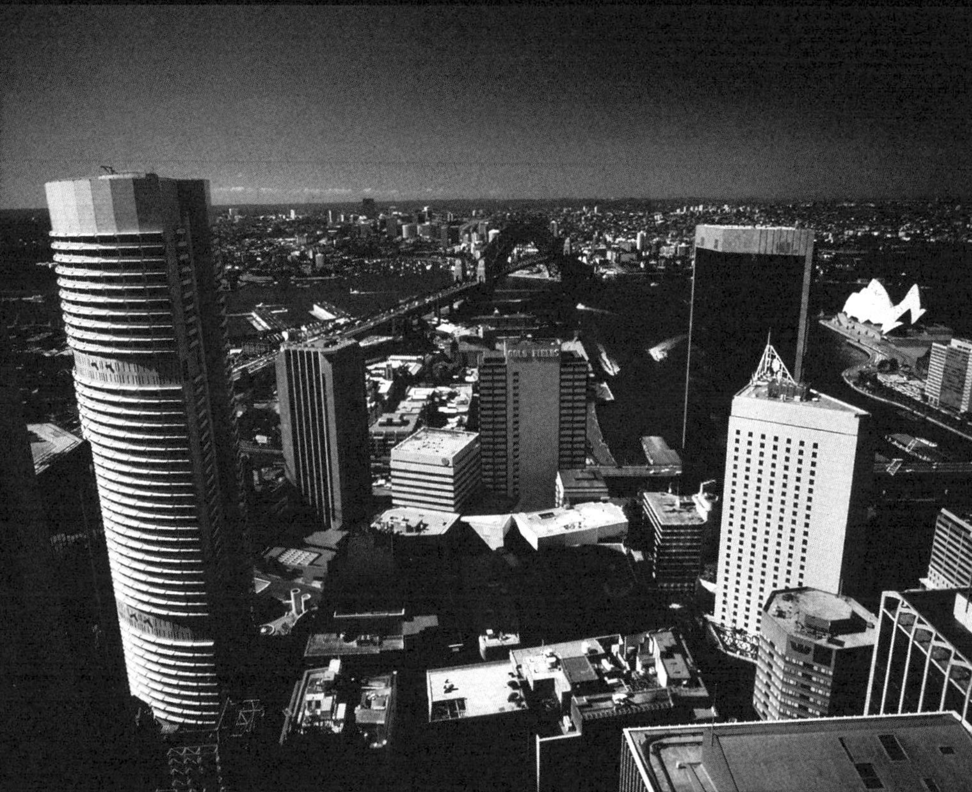

2.2

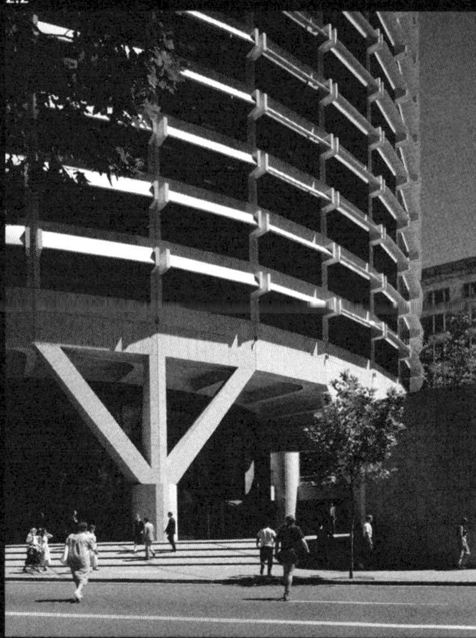

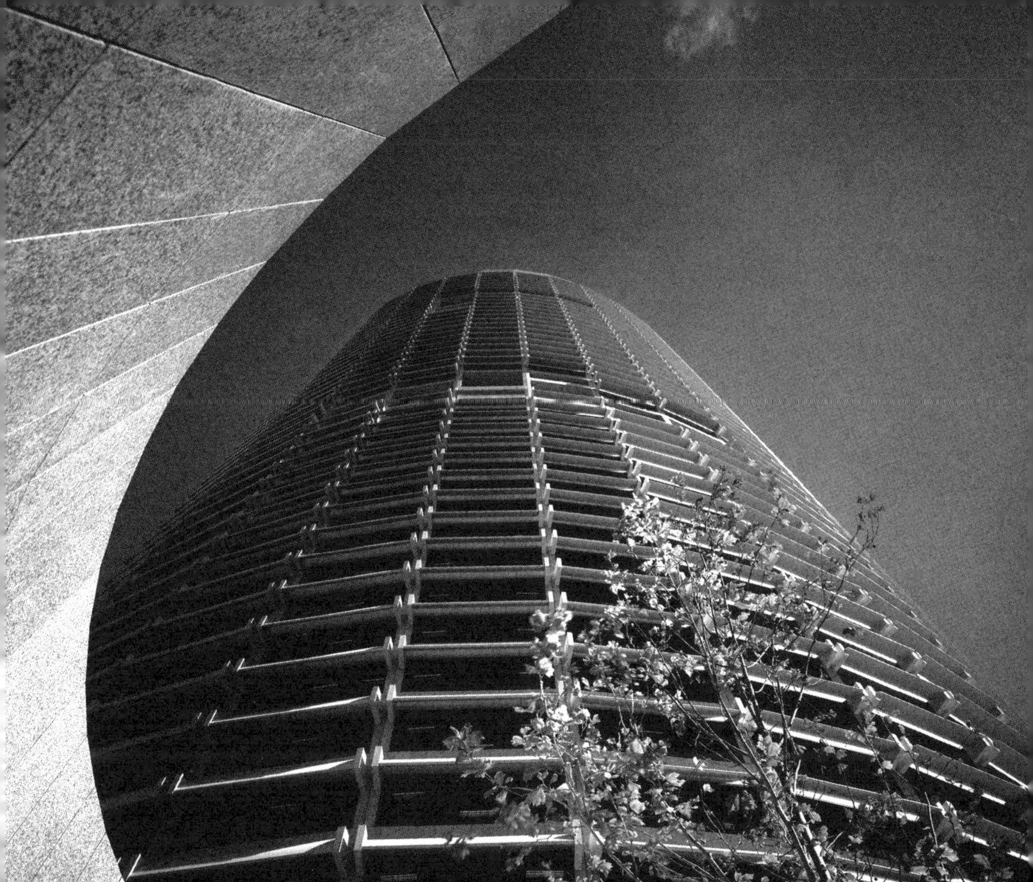

.3

Grosvenor Place, 1982–88

N D

D

E

3.1

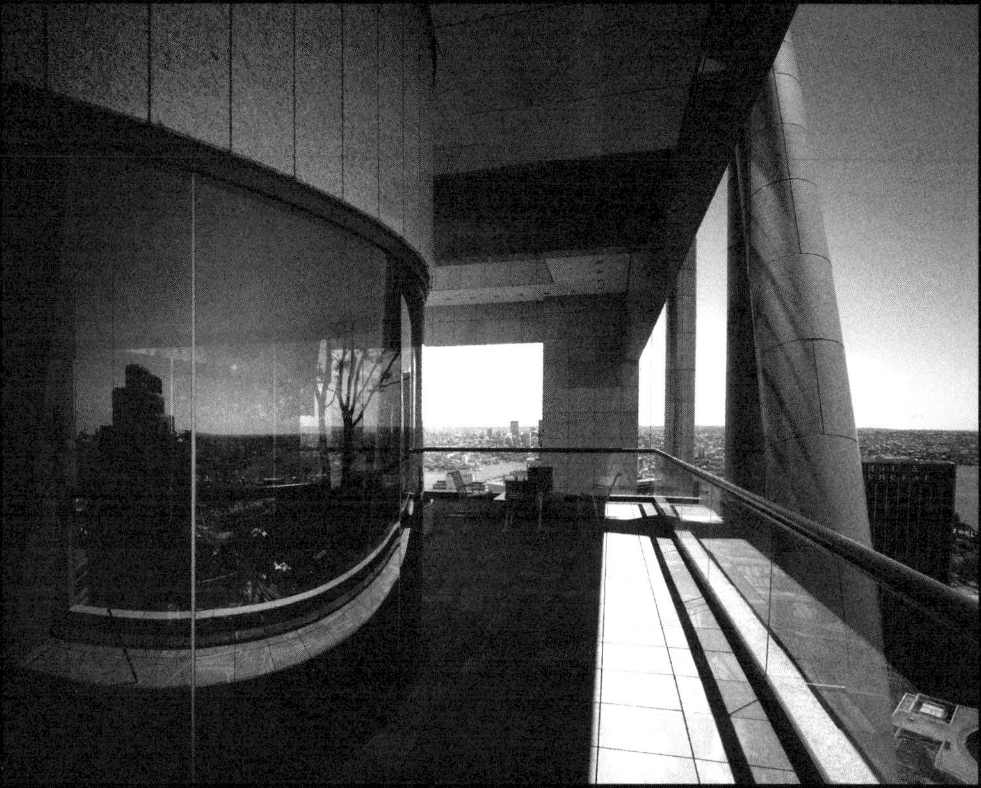

3.2

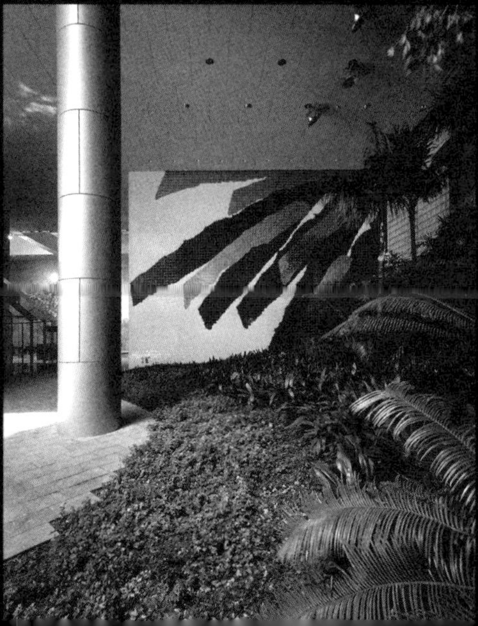

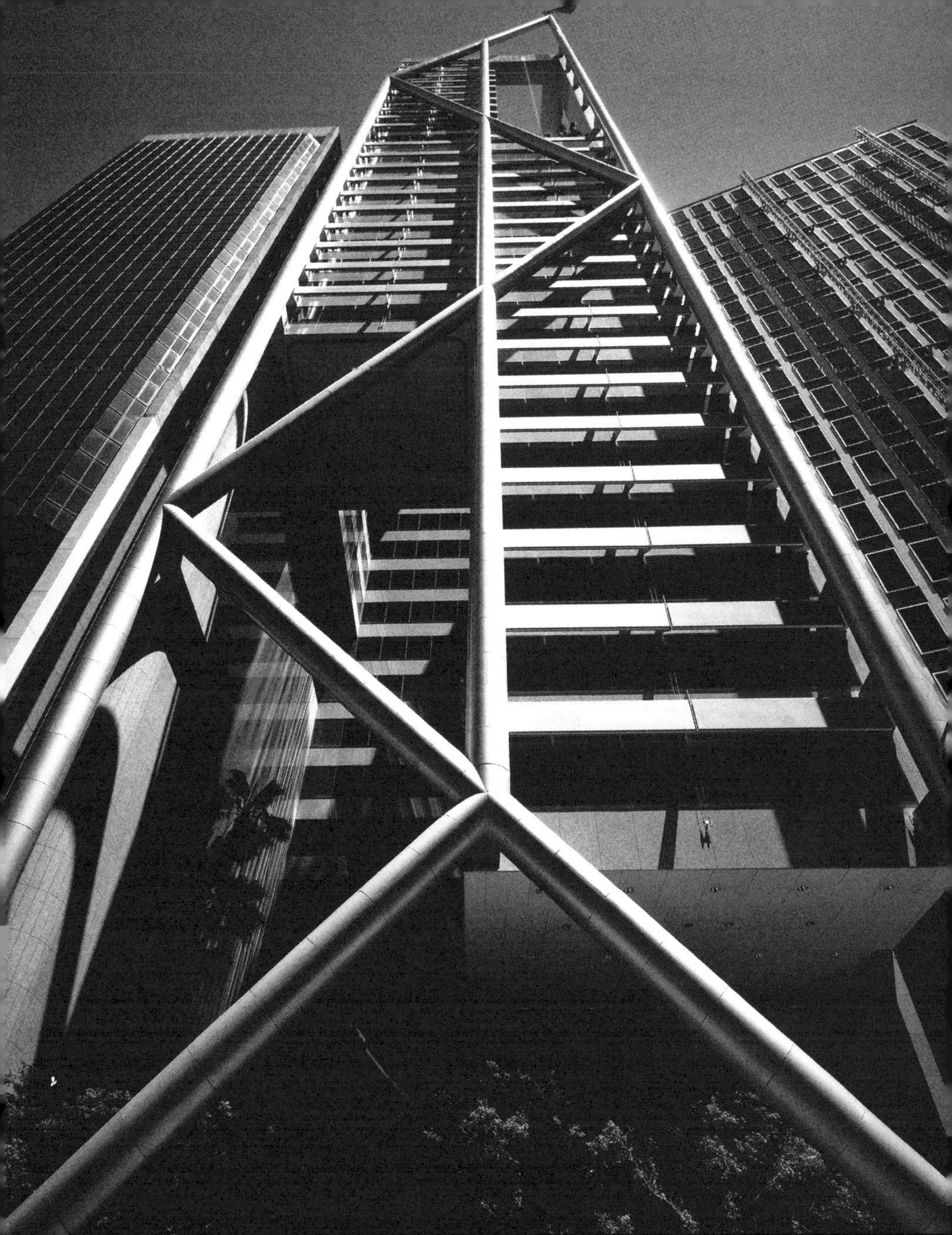

.3

Capita Centre, 9 Castlereagh Street, 1984–89

Expanded Architecture –
Temporal Spatial Practises

Contents

III Experimental Practice

IV Scholarly Discourse

V Appendix

I

TEMPORAL FORMAL AT SEIDLER CITY

Claudia Perren

In 2014 the curatorial project *Expanded Architecture* was devoted to the Australian architectural icons of modernism designed by Harry Seidler, examining current artistic perspectives on Bauhaus ideas and its advocates. Seidler is considered Australia's most renowned modernist architect, the person who brought the ideas and principles of international modernism "down under."

Born the son of a textile manufacturer in 1923 Vienna, Seidler's flight from the Nazis in 1938 first led him to England and then to Canada and the United States. At the Harvard Graduate School of Design in 1945, he met Bauhaus founder Walter Gropius, who had also emigrated, and became his student in the master's programme. During the Christmas break, Seidler worked in Alvar Aalto's Boston office. After graduation in 1946, he studied with former Bauhaus master Josef Albers at the legendary Black Mountain College, in North Carolina, and afterwards worked for Marcel Breuer and Oscar Niemeyer, other greats of modernism.

In 1948 Seidler went to Australia to design a residence for his parents. Located in remote bushland beyond suburban Sydney, the cubic Rose Seidler House—characterized by glass and a continuum of free standing planes—was the first building on the fifth continent for which modern methods of design and construction were so consistently pursued and implemented. Seidler decided to settle in Sydney and opened an architectural practice in 1949. After designing additional residential buildings based on Bauhaus ideas, he created Australia Square. It was the country's first building complex to combine office and retail spaces, large halls, and parking, thus merging private property with public space. The fifty-story skyscraper, which has a round floor plan, effectively altered the silhouette of Sydney and is to this day considered by many to be the most beautiful high-rise in Australia. It was also the start of his collaboration with the famous structural engineer Pier Luigi Nervi. Later, Seidler built a series of other buildings that shaped Sydney's cityscape: the MLC Centre, Grosvenor Place, Capita Centre, now 9 Castlereagh Street, and the Horizon Apartments. Seidler has also left his architectural mark in other Australian cities and in Europe, including the Australian embassy in Paris and social housing projects, like the Wohnpark Neue Donau, in Vienna.

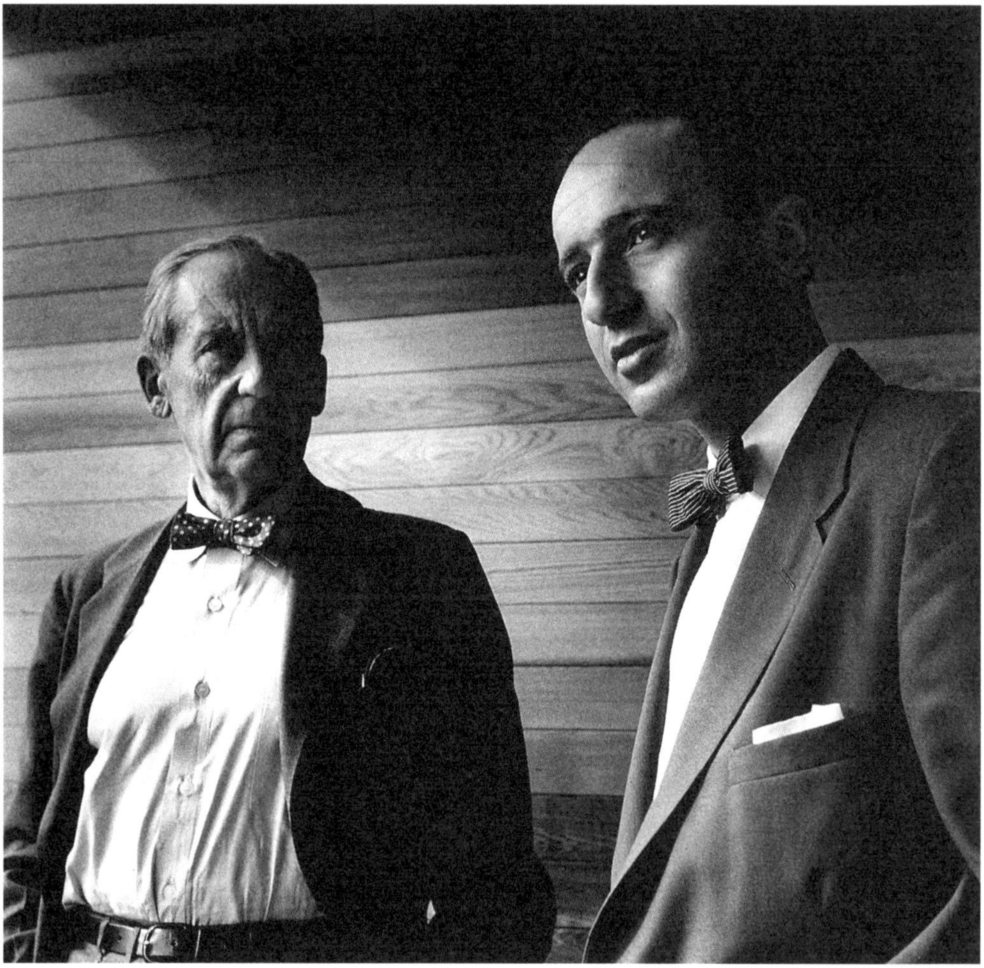

Pioneers of modernis ideas. Walter Gropius and Harry Seidler at Julian Rose House, Wahroonga, Sydney, Photo: Max Dupain, 1954.

With the exhibition *Temporal Formal at Seidler City,* Expanded Architecture focused on three iconic buildings by Seidler in Sydney's central business district, combining artistic experiments—cross-disciplinary and public interactions—with the architectural traces of modernism in Australia in temporary interventions. How can temporary artistic approches be used to think about and experience modern architecture in new and unexpected ways? For one night only, 7 November 2014, the lobbies of Australia Square (1965–67), Capita Centre (1984–89), and Grosvenor Place (1982–88) became the subject of artistic exploration and the scene for art installations, sound experiments, and performances. On the following day, a research symposium was held at the Museum of Sydney, where the exhibition *Harry Seidler: Painting toward Architecture,* co-curated by Vladimir Belogolovsky and Caroline Butler-Bowden, was being held. In this way, Expanded Architecture combined, through direct contact, contemporary artistic experimentation, public participation, and interdisciplinary scholarly discourse with modernist architectural cultural heritage.

For his buildings, Seidler often worked with such artists as Josef Albers, the American artists Norman Carlberg, Helen Frankenthaler, Sol LeWitt, Charles O. Perry, and Frank Stella, and the Danish artist Lin Utzon, often speaking of the parallels of his designs and their concepts and treatments of geometries and patterns. Against this backdrop, artists, designers, and architects were invited through an open call for works to explore spatial intersections of art and architecture in various periods, from the Bauhaus era to the modular art of the 1960s to contemporary approaches. Eleven site-specific works were selected and exhibited in the *Temporal Formal at Seidler City exhibition*. Documented in this book together with the results of the symposium mentioned above, they draw attention to the global legacies and multifaceted aspects of the Bauhaus heritage, highlighting its current relevance through contemporary artistic productions.

Scholarly Discourse

II

DEFINING THE EXPANDED

Sarah Breen Lovett

Since the 1960s, interdisciplinary crossovers amongst art, cinema, performance and architecture have been referred to as *expanded*. Thus, the title of this exhibition series, *Expanded Architecture*, was developed within the lineage of such practices as *expanded art, expanded cinema, the expanded field*, and *expanded spatial practices*. This paper will illustrate how the term *expanded* was first used in very specific ways, but then was broadly employed in a less-defined manner as the terminology became adopted, morphed and adapted to suit various interpretations. Rather than leading to the dilution of the original intention, the process of expanding the definition created multiple avenues for further definition, with ever-increasing richness in and a myriad of levels of inquiry to draw upon. Further this paper will ilustrate the avenues of inquiry associated with the term *expanded* do not imply expansion by moving away from the concerns of one's own discipline, but instead they offer an interrogation of one discipline by reframing it through another. To clarify this point we will now have a brief look at the different uses of the term expanded in interdisciplinary partices.

Expanded art was one of the first adaptations of the term *expanded* in relation to art practices. It can be traced back to 1946, in reference to an exhibition of paintings exploring new visual patterns in urban contexts, including "aerial views, cloverleaf highways, electric power lines, skyscrapers, giant airports and factories, a world of new scientific theories and processes, relativity, atomic power, radar, psychoanalysis, motion pictures and television."[1] It is interesting to note the aesthetic links between these works of *expanded art* and the early Bauhaus experiments in photography by László Moholy-Nagy.[2]

The term *expanded art* was then popularized by the Lithuanian-born American Fluxus artist George Macinuas in the mid-1960s through the "Expanded Arts Diagram."[3] In this diagram, the *expanded arts* are first viewed as encompassing a variety of practices, including verbal theatre, happenings, neo-baroque theatre, collage, *expanded cinema*, kinesthetic theatre, acoustic theatre, events/neo-haiku theatre, anti-arts, and political culture. From a second perspective, the diagram cites broadened use of *expanded art* as an umbrella term to include not only various types of media, but also assorted content, intents, and experiences. Evidenced through this diagram, the historical use of the term *expanded* was adapted to redefine the parameters of art practice.

Expanded cinema was coined in the 1950s by the American experimental filmmaker Stan Vanderbeek to describe multiple, shared cinematic experiences, whereby

1 Edith Weigle, "Expanded Art Exhibition," *Chicago Daily Tribune*, 17 June 1946, p.27.

2 Laszlo Moholy-Nagy, *Painting, Photography, Film*, trans. Janet Seligman (Cambridge, Mass., 1927).

3 George Maciunas, "Expanded Arts Diagram," *Film Culture: Expanded Arts*, no. 43 (1966), p. 7.

people in one cinematic space have the same experience as people in another cinematic space.[4] Ultimately, Vanderbeek saw *expanded cinema* as a device for communicating between cultures.[5] Beginning in the 1960s, as documented by Mekas, the term became used in reference to cinema mixed with performance-based mediums, happenings, and kinesthetic theatre.[6] Vanderbeek, however, dismissed this practice as inter-media, not *expanded cinema*, as the focus was not on intercultural exchange.[7] In 1970 the American theorist Gene Youngblood also defined *expanded cinema* by its inter-social implications: "When we say expanded cinema we mean consciousness ... man's ongoing historical drive to manifest his consciousness outside of his mind, in front of his eyes."[8]

Another faction of *expanded cinema* was created by British film artists' multiscreen, live-action events, including those by the group Filmaktion. Although these artists did not initially define their practice as *expanded cinema*, such influential film figures as the Lithuanian-born American film critic Jonas Mekas and the Austrian artist Peter Weibel did.[9] Stemming from a background in structural cinema, this form of *expanded cinema* was more focused on the processes of film-making and audiences' critical engagement, rather than the creation of spectacle or illusion. As British film theorist Jackie Hatfield notes, this type of *expanded cinema* aimed to interrogate the parameters of the discipline of cinema through "notions of conventional filmic language (for example dramaturgy, narrative, structure, technology) that are either extended or interrogated outside of the single-screen space."[10]

These artists are of particular interest because they engaged with architecture to examine a formal, structural type of *expanded cinema*.[11] As Mekas notes, "The London School is deep into structural researches, into process art, and formal explorations of space relationships."[12] The British artist Malcom Le Grice defined this type of *expanded cinema* as *formal expanded cinema* and compared it to *expanded cinema*, which aimed to create visual immersive projection environments that he called total *expanded cinema*.[13]

The formal and total approaches to *expanded cinema* outlined above are much more specific than the general contemporary understanding of *expanded cinema* as a variety of experimental film and projection practices that expand physically and visually beyond the frame of the screen and the traditional cinema framework. This broad understanding of the term is described in the contextual diagram of *expanded cinema* by Duncan White.[14] The diagram includes 1920s Bauhaus filmic experiments, 1960s happenings, as well as contemporary immersive interactive environments and internet art.

4 Mark Bartlett, "Socialimagestics and the Visual Acupuncture of Stan Vanderbeek's Expanded Cinema," *in Expanded Cinema: Art, Performance, Film*, ed. David Curtis et al. (London, 2011), p. 52.

5 Ibid., p. 54; Stan Vanderbeek, "Expanded Cinema: A Symposium, N.Y. Film Festival, 1966," *Film Culture: Expanded Arts*, no. 43 (Winter 1966), p. 1.

6 Jonas Mekas, *Movie Journal: The Rise of New American Cinema, 1959–1971* (New York, 1972), pp. 188–222.

7 Jonas Mekas, introduction, *Film Culture: Expanded Arts*, no. 43 (Winter 1966), p. 1.

8 Gene Youngblood, *Expanded Cinema* (New York, 1970), p. 41.

9 Malcolm Le Grice, "Around 1966," *Abstract Film and Beyond* (Cambridge, Mass., 1977), p. 121.

10 Jackie Hatfield and Stephen Littman, eds., *Experimental Film and Video: An Anthology* (Eastleigh, 2006), p. 237.

11 See Sarah Breen Lovett, "Expanded Architectural Awareness through the Intersection of Expanded Cinema and Architecture" (PhD diss., University of Sydney, forthcoming).

12 Jonas Mekas, "Movie Journal," *Village Voice*, 27 September 1973, 61.

13 Le Grice, "Around 1966," p. 122.

14 Duncan White, "Expanded Cinema," *Vertigo* 4, no. 2 (2009), https://www.closeupfilmcentre.com/vertigo_magazine/volume-4-issue-2-winter-spring-20091/expanded-cinema/ (accessed 21 May 2015).

Expanded field was coined by the American artist Robert Morris, but popularized by the American theorist Rosalind Krauss in 1979.[15] Both Morris and Krauss use the term to define a set of postmodern sculptural practices that extend beyond the plinth and context of the gallery. Krauss notes that artists of that time "operate directly on the frame of the world of art. The term *expanded field* is one way of mapping that frame."[16] According to Krauss, artists such as Morris, Carl Andre, Bruce Nauman, Richard Serra, and Robert Smithson established their work off the plinth and in context with their surroundings. In Krauss's Klein group diagram, the *expanded field* navigates the archipelago of architecture, non-architecture, landscape, and non-landscape. These elements are the chosen parameters, because in the quest for autonomy, modernist sculpture had rejected the context in which sculpture sat, such as landscape and architecture. It therefore became crucial to include them in creating a field for postmodern practices.[17] As the British theorist Jane Rendell says, sculpture, therefore becomes a practice suspended between a series of oppositions that categorize art practices not by their similarities but by their differences.[18] In this way the *expanded field* is defined as much by what it is as what it is not.

What is most significant about Krauss's *expanded field* for the development of *expanded architecture* is the way in which architecture is situated. The term *axiomatic structures* sits between architecture and non-architecture. Krauss describes this as "some kind of intervention into the real space of architecture, sometimes through spatial reconstruction."[19] She calls the American Nauman's *Live-Taped Video Corridor* (1967) "a process of mapping the axiomatic features of the architectural experience—the abstract conditions of openness and closure—onto the reality of a given space."[20] Today, the term *expanded field* is no longer used to refer only to sculpture in the context of architecture and landscape, but also to architecture and landscape in the context of art, writing, cultural conditions, and social networks. The intensity of disciplinary inquiry into the *expanded field* is, as the American historian Hal Foster has described it, an implosion, as opposed to an explosion, despite the appearance of an ever-expanding nature.[21] This is evidenced through interdisciplinary conferences, such as "Retracing the Expanded Field," where *there has been a constant working and reworking of the expanded field*.[22] *Expanded spatial practice* is arguably more closely linked to *expanded architecture* than the *expanded field*, because of its implied relationship to the spectator and situated-ness within various contexts. Rendell coined the term *expanded spatial practice* in 2009 as "an expanded consciousness of space: thinking and practicing space in an expanded sense might

15 As noted in Michael Archer, *Art since 1960*, World of Art (London, 1997), p. 94; Rosalind Krauss, "Sculpture in the Expanded Field," *October*, no. 8 (Spring 1979): 38.

16 Rosalind Krauss et al., *Art since 1900: Modernism, Antimodernism, Postmodernism* (London, 2004), p. 544.

17 Ibid., p. 543.

18 Jane Rendell, *Art to Architecture: A Place Between* (London and New York, 2006), p. 41.

19 Krauss, "Sculpture in the Expanded Field," p. 41.

20 Ibid.

21 Chrissie Iles, "Inside Out: Expanded Cinema and Its Relationship to the Gallery in the 1970s," in *Expanded Cinema: Activating the Space of Reception* (London, 2009); also see Foster, quoted in Jane Rendell, "Site-Writing: Critical Spatial Practice," paper presented at "Expanded Spatial Practices: A Symposium Exploring the Conditions and Possibilities for Cross-Disciplinary Approaches to Spatial Practice," 10–12 September 2009, p. 5.

22 Spyros Papapetros and Julian Rose, eds., *Retracing the Expanded Field* (Cambridge, Mass., 2006).

then place emphasis on interior spaces of the psyche as well as those external landscapes, but also on what it means to operate spatially ... establishing a relation between the two."[23] An *expanded spatial practice* could also be considered less politically and socially motivated than Rendell's other term, *critical spatial practice,* which she describes as work that has "spatial, temporal and social considerations."[24] In Rendell's definition of critical spatial practice, there is arguably a fine line between art that evokes an effect and art that critically engages with its disciplinary context.[25]

An interesting example of this delicate definition is Rendell's account of the material and phenomenological investigations of the French associates Jean-Gilles Decosterd and Philippe Rahm as critical spatial practice. Rahm's work is characterized by Rendell as questioning the parameters of its own discipline and not just the effect of a space.[26] Also of relevance is Rendell's description of critical spatial practice that is "at the edge of between and across different disciplines, ... adopting methods that call into question disciplinary procedures."[27] That is, the expanded nature of the inquiry is done specifically to interrogate the parameters of one's own discipline. Rendell offers the works of the British artists Tacita Dean and Jane and Louise Wilson as examples of self-reflexive and critical spatial practices that reframe understandings of architecture through filmic installation.[28] Foster describes contemporary art and architecture practices as post-critical. By this he means practices that do not situate themselves in terms of any critical inquiry and may have a heightened concern with "subjecthood." In relation to installation that engages with architecture, Foster wrote that a post-critical practice produces "spaces that confuse the actual with the virtual and/or with sensations that are produced as effects yet seem intimate, indeed internal, nonetheless."[29] Foster cites the works of the American artist James Turrell, Danish-Icelandic artist Olafur Eliasson, Swiss architects Jacques Herzog and Pierre de Meuron, and Phiippe Rahm as examples of post-critical practice. He argues that through these works, "the phenomenological reflexivity of 'seeing oneself see' approaches its opposite: an installation or a building that seems to do the perceiving for us."[30] Because *expanded architecture* focuses on a reflexivity of one's relationship to architecture, according to Foster's definition, it could be viewed as fetishizing the subjective experience of architecture through post-critical practice.

In summation, all the terms discussed above had various influences on the selection of the title *Expanded Architecture* for this exhibition series, situating it among this lineage of creative practices that questioned disciplinary parameters. There is evidence of two previous uses of the term *expanded architecture* that predate the *Expanded Architecture* series

23 Rendell, "Site-Writing," p. 7.

24 Rendell, *Art to Architecture,* p. 2.

25 Rendell, *Art to Architecture,* p. 101.

26 Ibid., pp. 54–56.

27 Ibid., p. 43.

28 Ibid., p. 85.

29 Hal Foster, "Post Critical," no. 139, October 2012, p. 7.

30 Ibid.

of exhibitions. The first was in 1966, in the American journal *Progressive Architecture,* where *"expanded architecture"* was used specifically to refer to the various experiments of designing architecture while under the influence of LSD.[31] The second example is from 1971, when a group of radical architects, including Superstudio and 9999 in Italy, adopted the term *expanded* in relation to architectural interventions and their notion of the Separate School for Expanded Conceptual Architecture.[32] To be considered *expanded architecture* today, in relation to this series of exhibitions, practices must be defined by an interrogation of the discipline of architecture.

This paper has illustrated that, despite the unarguable expansive connotations of the term *expanded,* when used in association with practices, it does not refer to an indefinite expansion into other disciplines.[33] Rather, it is used to refer to an internal and interdisciplinary interrogation of one's own discipline through the lens of other disciplines.[34] That is, *expanded architecture* questions what the parameters of architecture are and how they can be examined through other practices, such as installation, performance, moving image, sound art, and so on. Therefore, it is useful not to think of *expanded* as something that infinitely expands outward in *x, y,* and *z* dimensions, but perhaps infinitely in those of *y* and *z* shored up by the perimeters of *x*. It is an eternal expansion of depth into the unknown that can be considered infinitely richer than expanding in all directions. This is not to say the terminology will always be used in this way; in fact, to attempt to define, control, and monitor the term could potentially negate its very potential. It is hoped that if *expanded* continues to be used as a term, *expanded architecture* will shed new light on architecture, opening up new cracks in the wall to reveal and reconstruct our spatial, material, sensorial, mental, social, cultural, and metaphysical relationships to it in built form and as a discipline.

31 Jan Rowan, "L.S.D.: A Design Tool?" *Progressive Architecture,* August 1966, pp. 147–153; Jan Rowan, "Expanding Architecture," *Progressive Architecture,* September 1966, pp. 185–187.

32 9999 and S-Space, *Vita, morte e miracoli dell'architettura = Life, Death and Miracles of Architecture* (Florence, 1971).

33 *Oxford English Dictionary,* 2nd ed. (Oxford, 2010), 261.

34 The disciplinary context refers to the quotidian surroundings of a discipline. It can be broadly interpreted as social and cultural influences, but more specifically the context consisting of medium, space, and spectator relations.

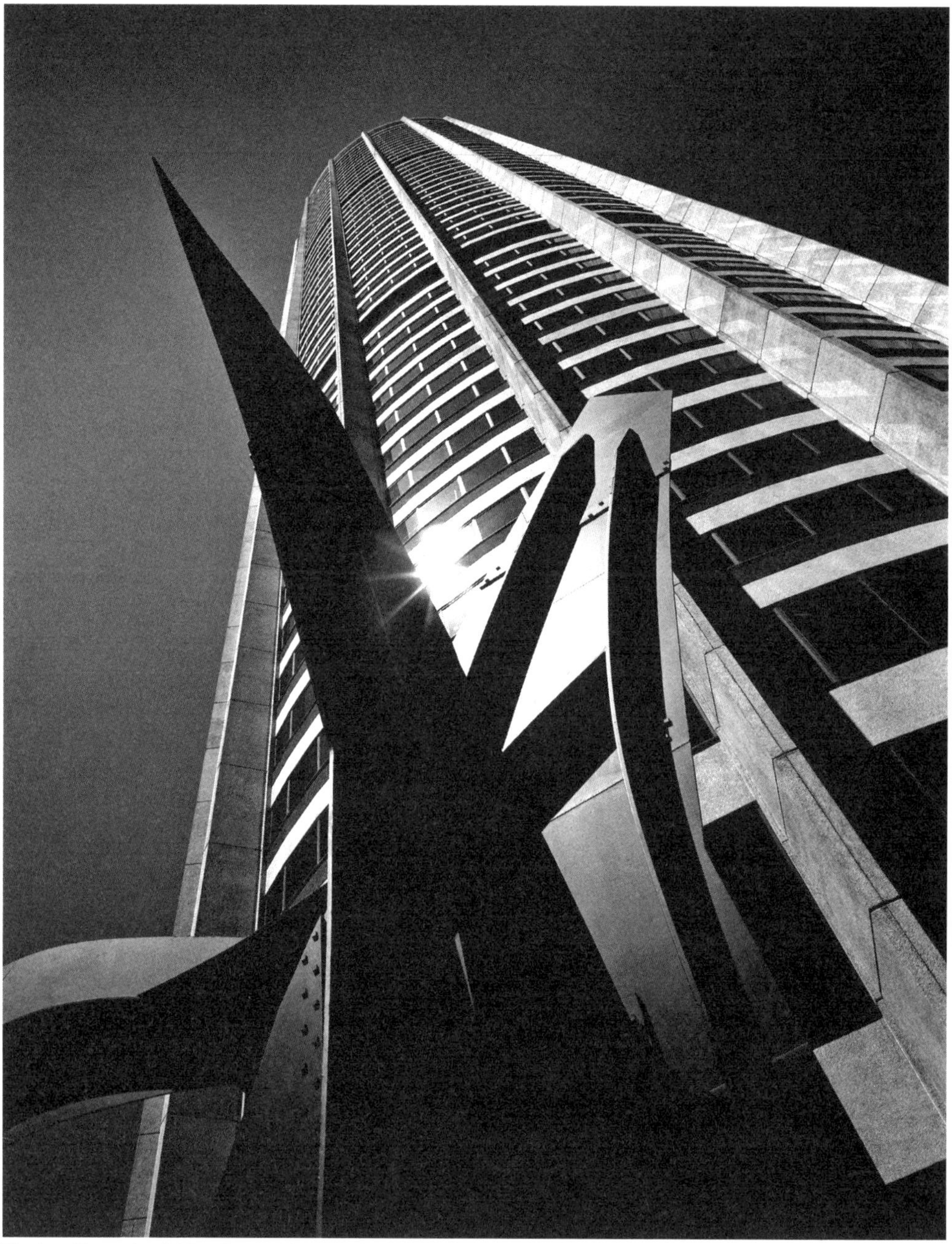

Fig. 1 Alexander Calder, *Crossed Blades*, 1967, Australia Square, Photo: Max Dupain, 1968.

BUILDINGS THAT EXPAND ARCHITECTURE

Vladimir Belogolovsky

No single building can be seen as dominating central Sydney today. There are many medium-height and tall towers standing closely, comprising a compact, thriving urban core, but nothing effectively attracts attention due to its size, height, materials, or form apart from the giant arc of the Harbour Bridge and the white shells of Jørn Utzon's Opera House, both pushed to the city's edges. Architecture simply dissipates into a fussy, neutral background for the daily routine of bustling commerce and streams of vehicular and pedestrian traffic that animate the narrow streets of Sydney's central business district, at least during business hours. Regardless, some buildings do stand out more than others. Among them, one must count the solid-looking and geometrically expressive towers designed by the visionary late modernist Harry Seidler, Australia's most prominent architect of the twentieth century. Seidler's distinguished career flourished Down Under for almost six decades, as evidenced by a total of seventy buildings and houses in Sydney, that is, Seidler City.

Seidler's prominence, however, is not based on sheer quantity alone. Many of his buildings were conceived and crafted by the architect as integral works of art, elevating the quality of the urban environment to the highest level. Three Seidler skyscrapers—Australia Square (1961–67), Grosvenor Place (1982–88), and Capita Centre, 1984–89 (now 9 Castlereagh Street)—were chosen to host the 2014 exhibition *Expanded Architecture: Temporal Formal at Seidler City*, featuring spatio-temporal installations, performances, and sound projects. This choice of buildings is fitting because one would be hard pressed to find another architects' work that embodies such a complete fusion of architecture, art, and technology.

The Australia Square tower was completed six years before the Opera House, becoming the first Australian skyscraper and the first truly modern icon on the continent. An architectural writer, Mark Wakely, recalled his first visit to the tower at the age of twelve with his father: "Until that day, for me, the world was about boring rectangles. The idea that a building could be circular had never entered my consciousness. Dad and I must have circled that entrance lobby half a dozen times, just delighting in the playfulness of it all."[1] Another fan, the photographer Patrick Bingham-Hall, called the tower "Australia's finest tall building, a perfect resolution of rational geometry, structural ingenuity and heroic form."[2]

1 Stephen Lacey, "Top of the Town," *Sunday Morning Herald*, 15 May 2004.

2 Patrick Bingham-Hall, *Austral Eden: 200 Years of Australian Architecture* (1999).

Australia Square was the first opportunity for Seidler to elevate an architectural project to an art form. It also began his long-lasting collaboration with the Italian engineer Pier Luigi Nervi, famous for his long-span, reinforced concrete structures. Nervi's contribution was twofold—designing the curved, interlocking ribs in the ceilings of the two lower floors for additional load bearing capacity and making the twenty exterior piers around the circumference taper toward the building's top to reflect that the columns carry lighter loads as they rise. These brilliant solutions, based on static laws of nature, make the tower remarkably graceful. Its magnificent ceiling ribs may be governed by as many logical explanations as any engineer could present, but it is their sheer beauty that makes visitors tilt their heads upward to view this eloquent building from its base all the way to its pointed top. One has to agree with Sydney architectural historian and critic Philip Drew when he marveled at Nervi's structural magic, asserting, "Sometimes it is difficult, if not impossible, to decide where considerations of statics leave off and aesthetics begin."[3]

Australia Square was just the beginning for the young architect whose work on this tower leapt to a completely new level. It was not surprising that Seidler's first skyscraper took the shape of a perfect circle or, to be precise, a twenty-sided polygon. The tower demonstrated Seidler's fascination with the geometry of a circle on a grand scale and in its purest form. After this tower, with each new project his plans grew in complexity, but it is this initial exploration of circular geometry that may have contributed to producing Seidler's "finest tall building." This perception can be attributed, at least in part, to the incredibly powerful image of the tower captured by the photographer Max Dupain (1911–92).

Surrounded by rectangular buildings built to the street line, the cylindrical tower occupies just a quarter of its site, making the overall perception of its mass both commendable and suitable by avoiding canyon-like spaces and allowing more light onto the surrounding streets. The setting evokes metaphorically and visually the famous renaissance painting *Ideal City,* by Piero della Francesca (ca. 1470, Galleria Nazionale delle Marche, Urbino). The proper balance is achieved here, as the chaos of the hustle and bustle of the modern city confronts pure harmony composed of dignifying platonic geometry. Seidler's desire to build a geometrically ideal tower, at least subconsciously, can perhaps be traced back to the biblical Tower of Babel, which most sources lead us to believe had a circular appearance.

Australia Square's ground-floor lobby originally featured the large Le Corbusier tapestry *UNESCO* (Fig. 2).[4] Due to the tapestry's deterioration, in 2003, following a major renovation of the building, it was auctioned off and replaced with a multicoloured round metal mural by Sol LeWitt (Fig. 3).

3 Philip Drew, *Two Towers: Harry Seidler—Australia Square, MLC Centre* (Sydney, 1980).

4 The wool tapestry, one of three copies, was executed by the Pinton Frères workshops in Aubusson, France, in 1956, based on a cartoon by Le Corbusier. The original Australia Square tapestry is now on view at the Sydney Conservatorium of Music, University of Sydney. The other two tapestries are in Paris and Zurich.

This pulsating, brightly coloured work accentuates the most beautiful features of the building and complements its strong character. The building itself is counterbalanced by the exuberant stabile *Crossed Blades* (1967) (Fig. 1), by Alexander Calder, positioned immediately outside. The black steel sculpture was the result of a personal collaboration with the artist. Seidler took part in such decisions as the sculpture's size, colour, material, and placement. Apart from major artworks by Calder and LeWitt at the ground level, the building's executive areas (Fig. 4) feature a sculpture of Norman Carlberg's serie *Positive-Negative* (1966), tapestries by Le Corbusier and Joan Miró, and the large tapestry *Yellow Summer* (1966), by the Australian artist John Olsen. The architect often commissioned these and many other artists to create a totality of spatial experience outside and inside his buildings.

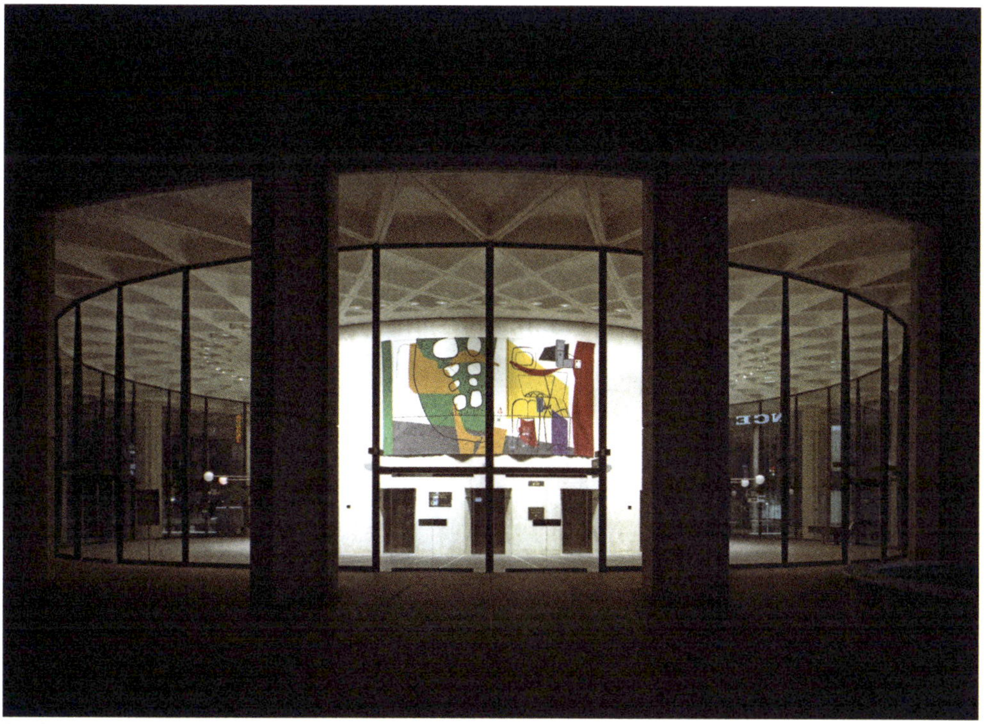

Fig. 2 Le Corbusier, Tapestry *UNESCO, 1956,* Lobby of Australia Square, Photo: Max Dupain, 1968.

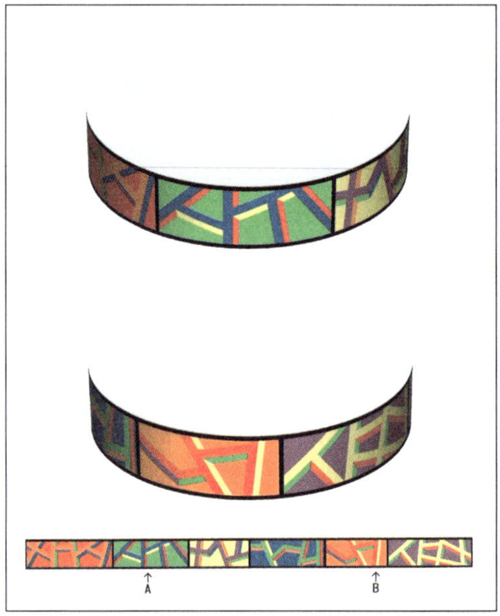

Fig. 3 Drawing for Sol LeWitt's multicoloured, round metal mural *Bars of Colour*, 2002 (installed 2003).

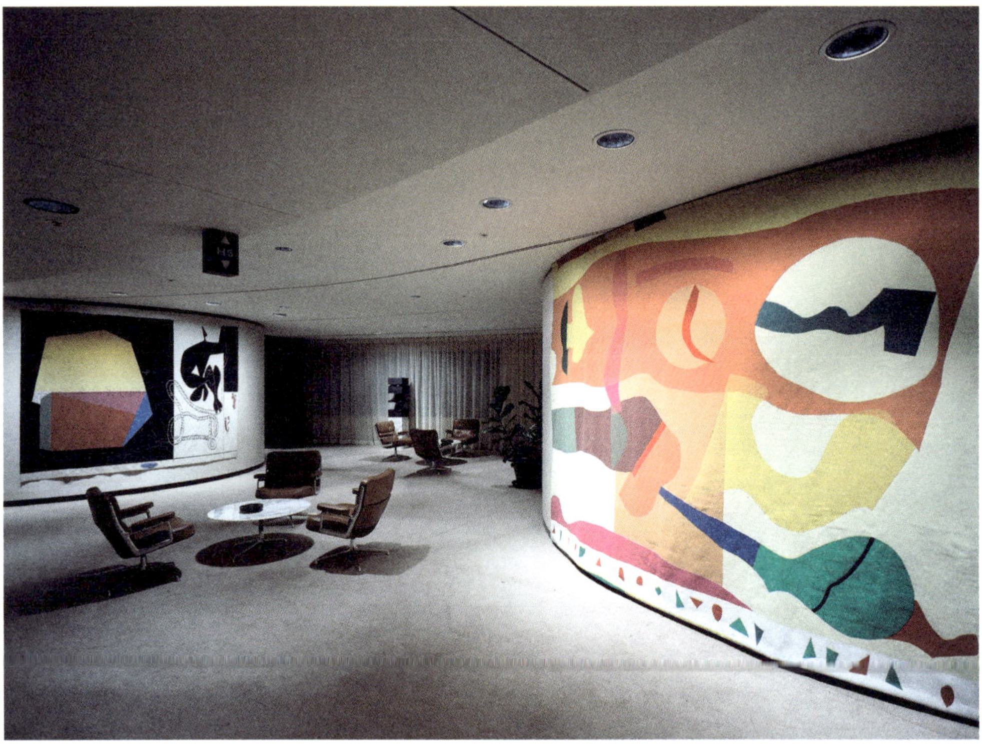

Fig. 4 Executive area featuring a sculpture of the serie *Positive-Negative*, 1966, by Norman Carlberg, (left) *Traces de pas dans la nuit*, 1957, by Le Corbusier, and (right) *Yellow Summer*, 1966, by John Olsen, Australia Square, Photo: Max Dupain, 1968.

Grosvenor Place stands as a grand curving gesture (Fig. 5), effectively visible from the harbour and masterfully adorned with a sweep of variably inclined fixed, aluminium sunshades, angled according to the sun's daily path. The building's plan is based on the geometry of two opposing quadrants slightly offset to better fit the site (Fig. 6). The quadrants serve as column-free office wings that embrace the elliptical core containing the elevator banks.

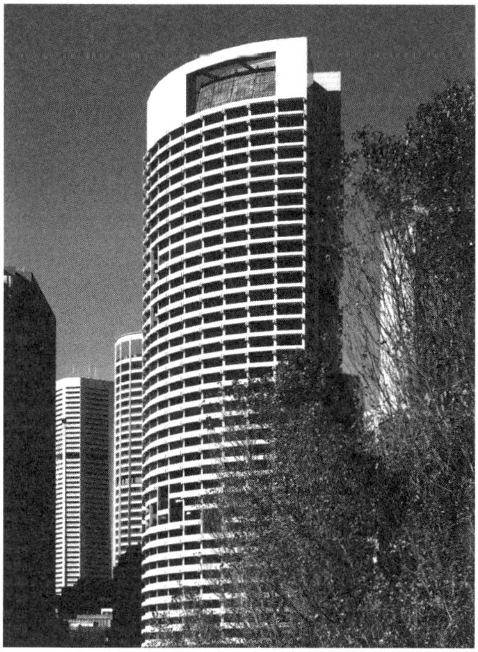

Fig. 5 *Grosvenor Place,* street view, in the background MLC Centre (left), and Australia Square (centre), Photo: Max Dupain 1989.

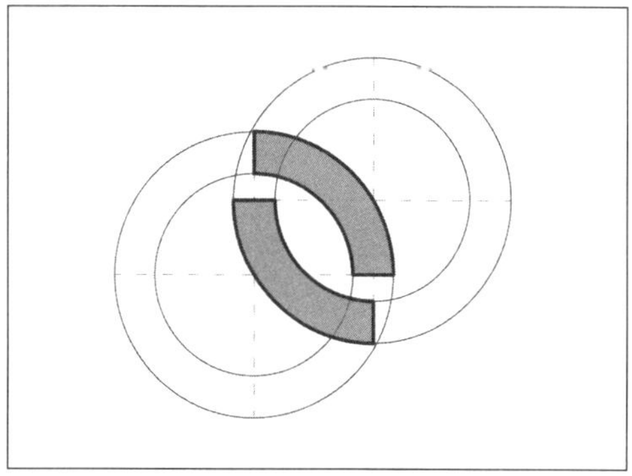

Fig. 6 Harry Seidler & Associates, *Grosvenor Place*, diagrammatic plan generated by two opposing quadrants, 1992.

The building, however, is more than a beautiful container. It is itself based on the same geometric principles as the artworks that the architect favored. In his quest to enrich architecture with fluid and plastic qualities, Seidler was consistently inspired by the artists Norman Carlberg (Fig. 7) and Charles O. Perry along with Frank Stella, with whom he shared an infatuation with circular geometry. The building's plan was influenced by Stella's *Protractor* series (1967–71), which was inspired by and based on the shape of a protractor: a straight edge and a semicircle. Stella's influence—in particular the patterns of the paintings *Flin Flon III, Flin Flon VIII*, and *Tahkt-I-Sulayman I*—is direct (Figs. 8 and 9). They pulsate intensely with the pull-push effect of overlapping and interlacing bands of bright colours, "interlaces, rainbows, and fans," as Stella calls them. No matter how complex or flamboyant these paintings might appear, they rely on a repetition of protractors (semicircles), quadrants, and other segments of a circle.

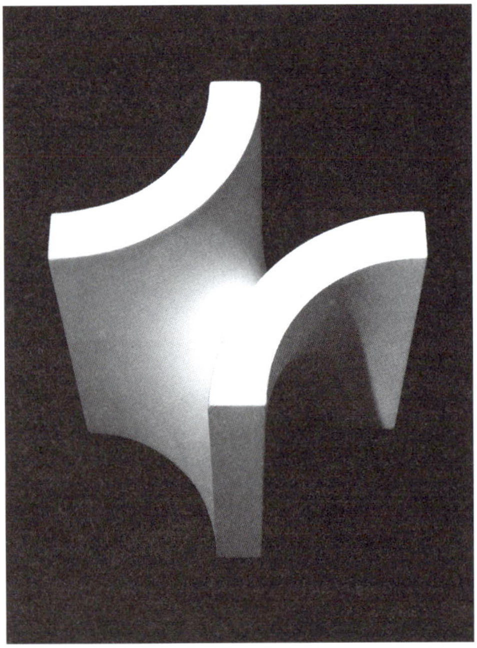

Fig. 7 Norman Carlberg, *Untitled,* (opposing quadrant) saddle shape modular unit, sculpture component, 1963–64, Photo: Harry Seidler, ca. 1965–73.

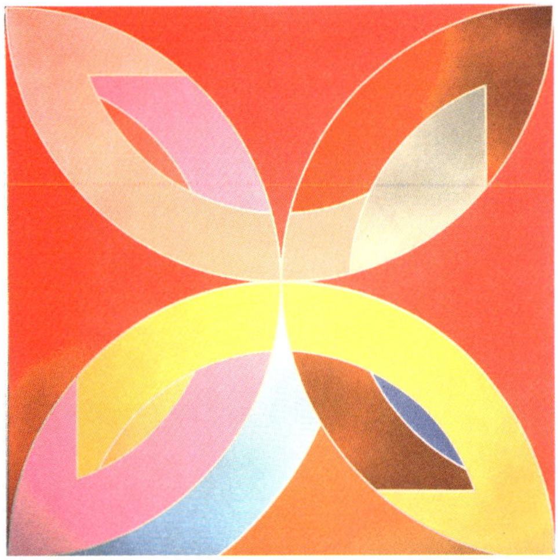

Fig. 8 Frank Stella, *Flin Flon III*, acrylic on canvas, 1969.

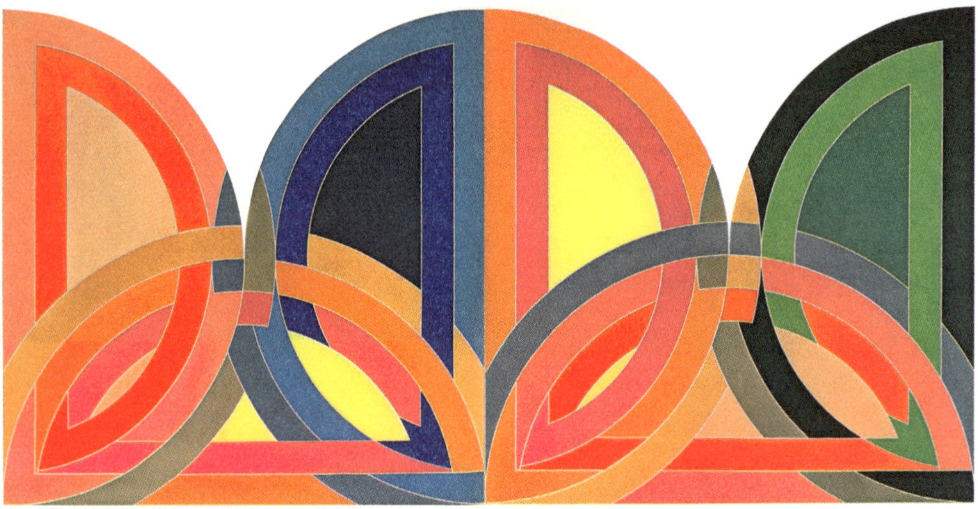

Fig. 9 Frank Stella, *Takht-i-Sulayman I*, synthetic polymer paint on canvas, 1967, Museum of Modern Art, New York.

It was this geometry of a circle that Seidler adapted for his architectural plans, as it was inherently suitable for mass production: A circle is based on repetitive conditions, whereas a rectangle or a square requires special corner conditions. This economy of means was reflected in the architect's main mission—to achieve maximum effect with minimum effort. Seidler's compositions are almost always resolved in plans that are then extruded vertically without further complications. It is the juxtaposition of curves in various horizontal planes that produces the spatial complexity required when these buildings are experienced in real life.

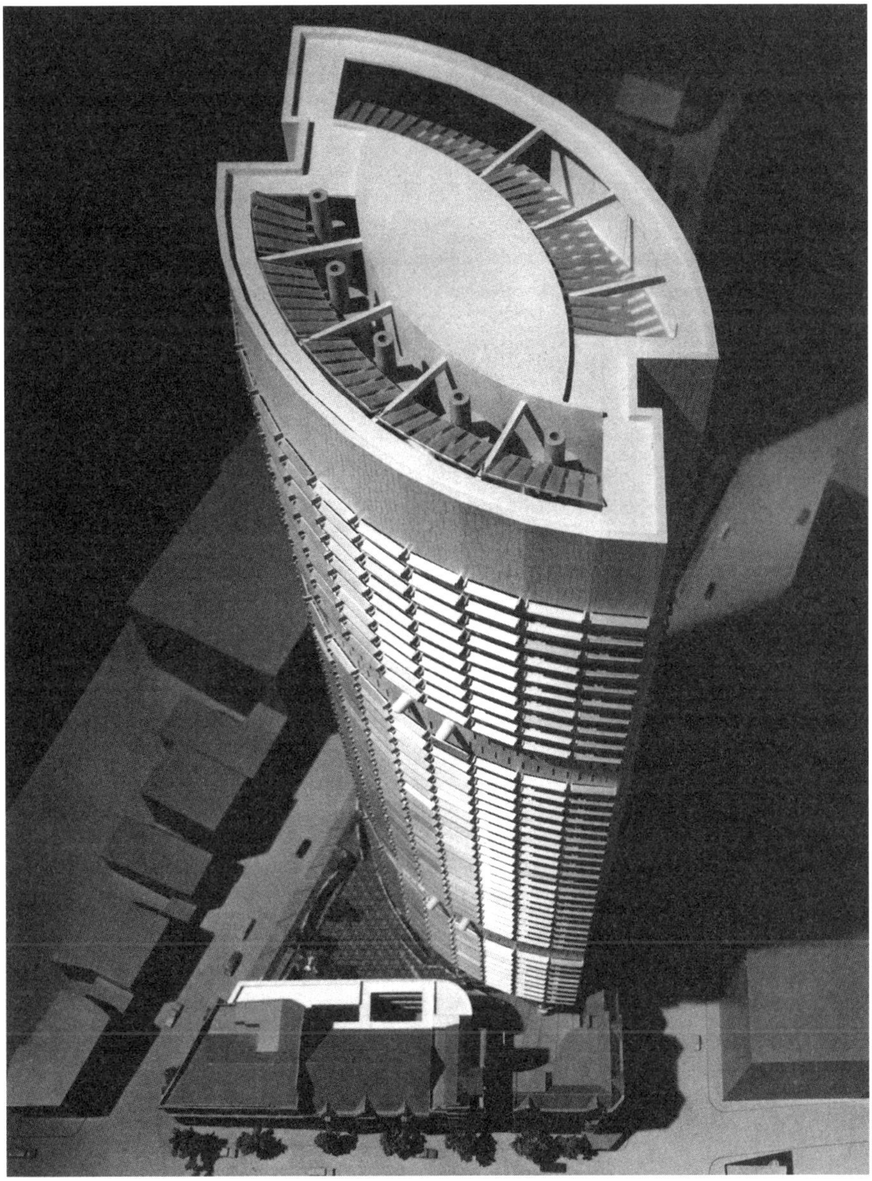

Fig. 10 *Grosvenor Place*, model by Bob Brown showing the effective volume achieved by the straight-forward extrusion of two opposing quadrants, Photo: Max Dupain, 1982.

Interestingly, while the building's design has parallels with Stella's early work, its lobby wall features very different paintings by him—*Cones and Pillars*, three large, deep, and multicoloured collage reliefs commissioned by the architect (Fig. 11). These paintings are part of the artist's series created between 1984 and 1987, when Grosvenor Place was still in the design stage. Stella painted them in New York—using oil paint on magnesium, an effect that allowed the surface to be etched to provide a distinctive sculptural quality—and they were then shipped to Sydney. They remain the most prominent examples of Stella's work in Australia.

Unlike the other two freestanding buildings, the Capita Centre is squeezed into an unusually deep and narrow rectangular site surrounded on three sides by buildings twenty-five to thirty storeys high. Admission of adequate natural light to the narrow site was made possible by including a full-height central atrium to serve as a light well. The atrium consists of staggered rectangular volumes with floating sky gardens of large trees and shrubs, all visible from the street, and the landscaped open-air lobby on the ground floor (Fig. 12).

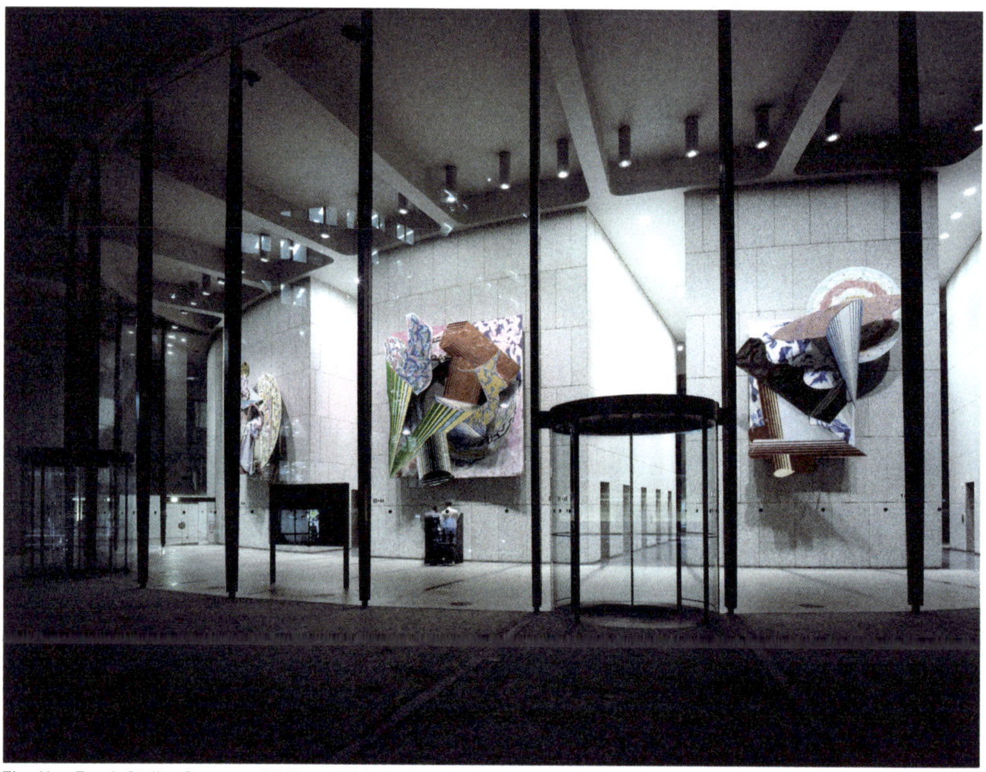

Fig. 11 Frank Stella, *Cones and Pillars*, 1984–87, installed at Grosvenor Place, Photo: Max Dupain, 1989.

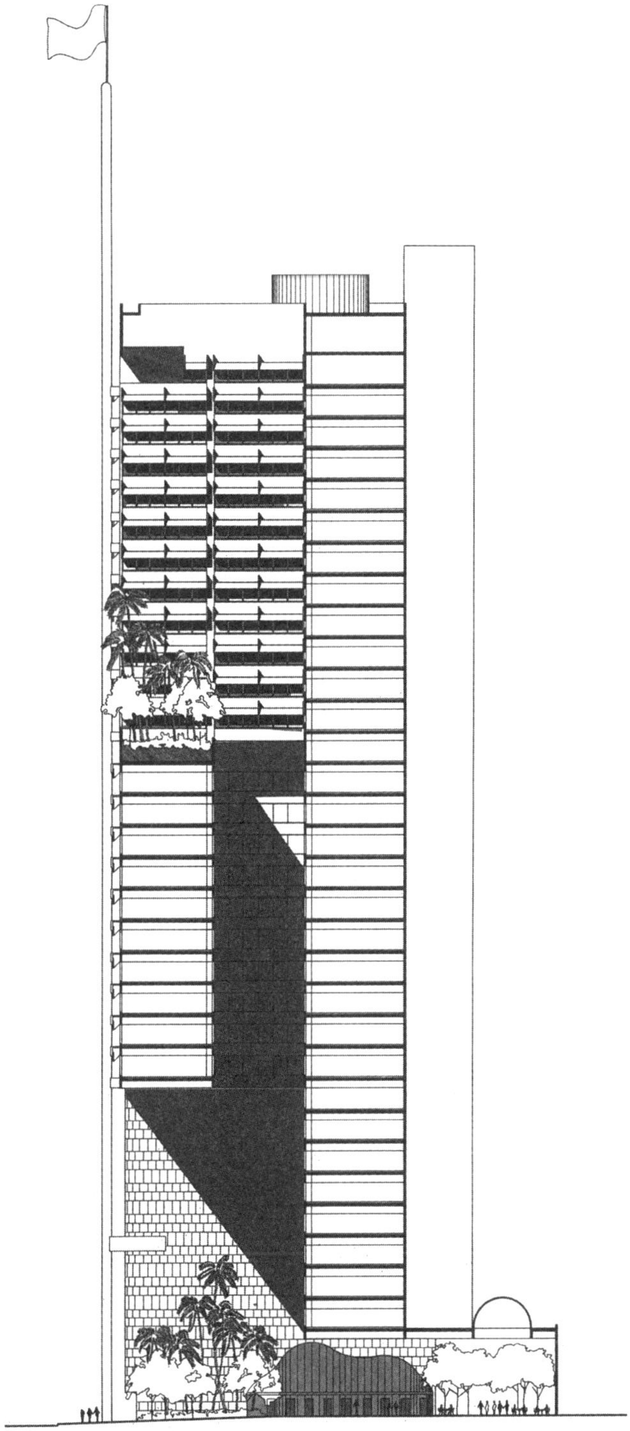

Fig. 12 Harry Seidler & Associates, *Capita Centre*, 9 Castlereagh Street. Section through the building showing full-height central atrium / light well with floating sky gardens, 1985.

The unusual hollowing of the tower created a dignified civic space, but it naturally caused a laterally unstable structural condition across the street façade that required strengthening the building through diagonal steel bracing (Figs. 13). The truss's structure is carried above the roofline to form a mast, a recognizable feature on the city's skyline. Apart from the heroic spire and the soaring atrium, the focus here is on a large ceramic mural created in 1989 by the Danish artist Lin Utzon, the daughter of Jørn Utzon (see endpaper images, fig. 3.2). Lin collaborated on a number of projects with Seidler throughout his career. The architect saw her lyrical forms "as essential in animating the intricate geometries of the architecture." The mural was made in Denmark, and the artist travelled to Sydney to install it.

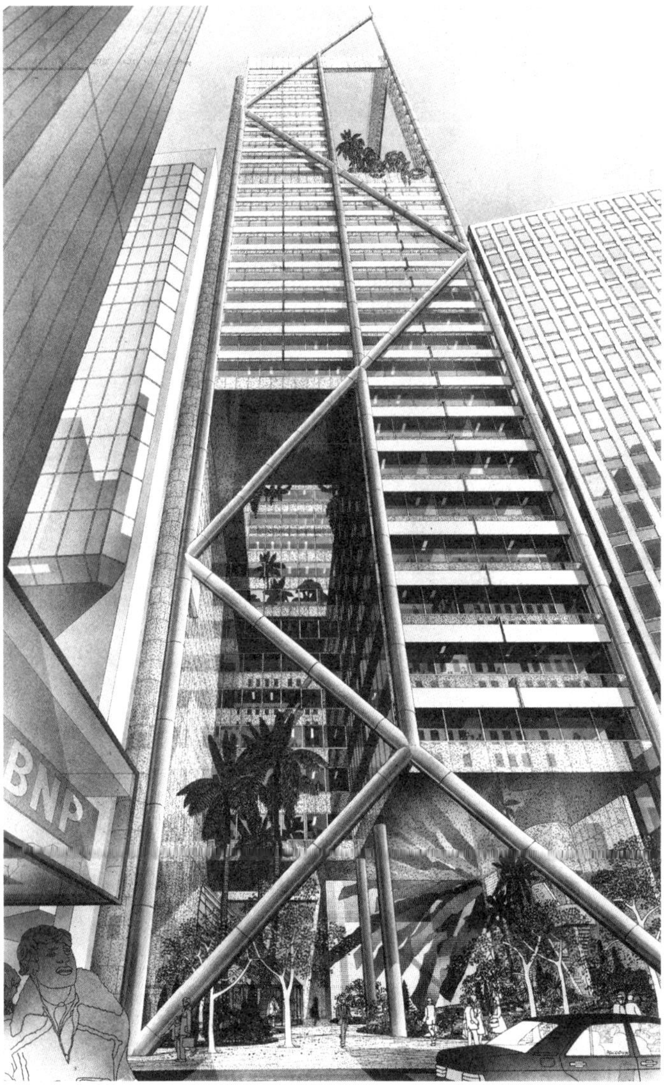

Fig. 13 Helmut Jacoby for Harry Seidler & Associates, *Drawing of Capita Centre*, 9 Castlereagh Street, 1985.

The building also features an extensive art collection selected by the architect. There is a bronze sculpture by Charles O. Perry, furniture by Marcel Breuer, and another mural by Utzon at the reception area of the executive floor (Fig. 14).[5] According to Seidler, Capita Centre was his most satisfying public project. This must have been because of the numerous challenges the architect had to overcome to create a meaningful and artistically striking work of architecture.

Looking back at Seidler's buildings brings to light many common threads, but their direct extension as inspiring works of art is the one that makes his creations truly memorable and emotional experiences. These works inspired the architect, and now his building environments inspire artists whose installations expand architecture.

5 Utzon's reception mural is now owned by Penelope Seidler and installed at the Seidler penthouse in Milson Point NWS. It was on view at the Museum of Sydney during the exhibition *Harry Seidler: Painting toward Architecture,* 1 November 2014–8 March 2015.

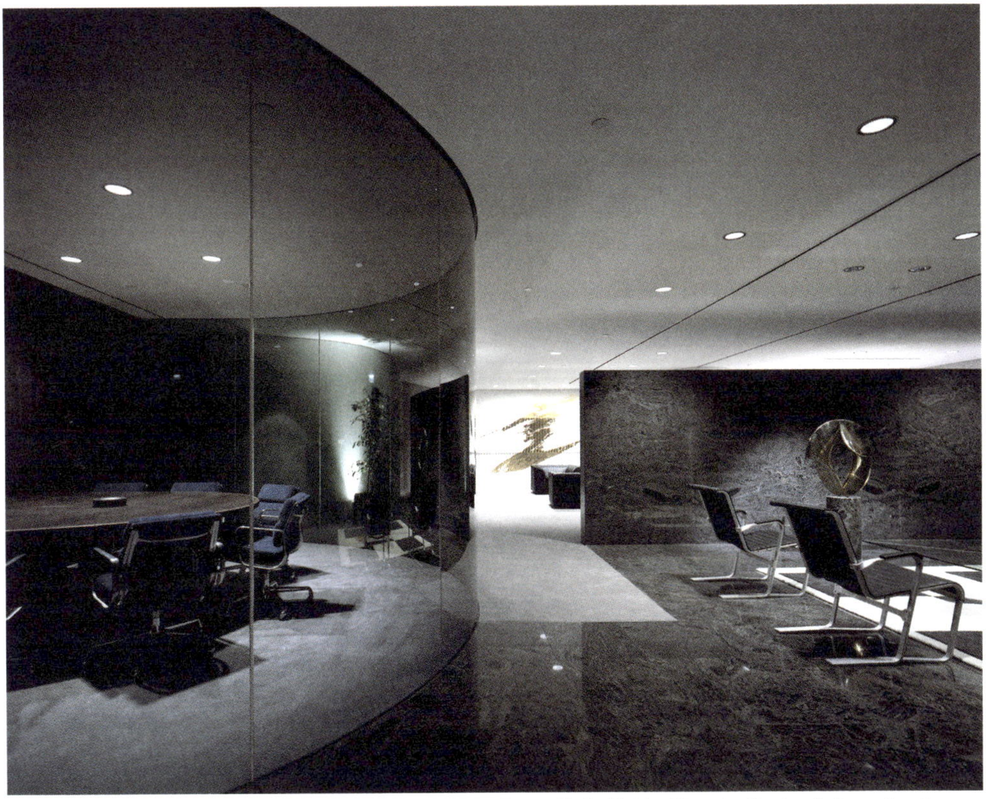

Fig. 14 Executive floor reception area with the bronze sculpture *Helix Mobius Mace* by Charles O. Perry, furniture by Marcel Breuer, and mural *Capita 2* by Lin Utzon, Capita Centre, 9 Castlereagh Street, Photo: Max Dupain, 1989.

SIX LECTURES: RECONSTRUCTING AND TESTING HARRY SEIDLER'S 1980s ARCHITECTURE DESIGN STUDIO

Paola Favaro

In 1980 the Austrian-born Sydney architect Harry Seidler (1923–2006) was appointed visiting professor in architecture at the University of New South Wales (UNSW). In March and June of that year, he became involved in the architecture graduation studio, where he coordinated and taught for a project to design a new building for the university's School of Architecture. Part of his academic commitment included delivering six lectures on the *guiding and motivating forces* of art and technology, the underpinnings of successful architectural design. In 1981 the UNSW School of Architecture published the outcome of his work as *Seidler Studio: A Record of Student Work under Harry Seidler*.[1] This paper explores Seidler's 1980 lectures, his approach to teaching architectural design (and its theoretical underpinnings), the influence of his American and European educational experience, and the impact of the Six Lectures on the 1980 architecture graduation studio.

Seidler embraced two principles: spatial imagination and technological innovation coupled with constructional logic, which he believed could achieve a higher level of design, especially if they were guided by influential modernist artists, architects, and engineers. A comprehensive analysis of Seidler's work is beyond the scope of this paper, but by analyzing his lectures one can better understand his work and design principles. In 2014, thirty-four years after Seidler's lectures, they were revisited in the context of the third year architecture graduation studio, wherein students were encouraged to watch the recorded lectures, read the transcriptions of them, and participate in a series of lunchtime lectures and discussions during which academics and professionals introduced or responded to three of Seidler's lectures and posed the question What can we learn from them?

The Six Lectures

Seidler's lectures were recorded by UNSW closed-circuit television from 10 April to 27 June 1980.[2] They ranged between seminar discussions and illustrated talks on specific themes and relations between modern architecture, art, and technology. Indeed, the topics were varied:

Lecture 1	"Interaction: Architecture and the Visual Arts"
Lecture 2	"Form Relations in Baroque and Modern Architecture, Part 1"

1 Harry Seidler, "The Programme," in *Seidler Studio: A Record of Student Work under Harry Seidler*, ed. Russell Jack (Sydney, 1981), p. 3.

2 The videotapes and their transcriptions are available on the UNSW Built Environment website as "Harry Seidler Lectures on Architecture (1980)," https://www.be.unsw.edu.au/content/watch-harry-seidler-lectures-architecture-1980. The tapes and their transcripts and slide lists are also available on YouTube: https://www.youtube.com/watch?v=I2TfN_NPXrc&list=PLMKtooDEad31WQAtOWmYwY1FZ0YOC2Q7I. UNSW Built Environment is extremely thankful to Mitchell Library at State Library of New South Wales holding this items in its Harry Seidler collection and making a copy for Polly Seidler who then made available the the digitised videotapes and Harry Seidler's slide lists, as the originals could not be found in the UNSW Library archive.

Lecture 3	"Consequence of Design and Detail"
Lecture 4	"Form Relations in Baroque and Modern Architecture, Part 2"
Lecture 5	"Habitat: Its Detail and Totality"
Lecture 6	"Principles in the Mainstream of Modern Architecture"

These should be understood in the context of the milieu in which Seidler operated, especially his involvement in education and collaborative work with the protagonists of the modern movement.

Seidler introduced two main design propositions of spatial imagination and constructional logic that clarify his belief in the guiding and motivating forces of art and technology and characterize successful architectural design. His two injunctions to students were that they strive for spatial imagination, to be achieved through visual education, and that they strive for constructional logic, which could be learned by understanding the technological innovation during the modernist period. In accordance, in the first instance, spatial imagination, he introduced the work of painters and sculptors from the modernist period and the work of Italian and German architects from the baroque era (1650–1750), exploring the way they used art and architecture in the context of space. By borrowing specific visual and geometric propositions, such as *channeling of vistas, asymmetry, dematerialization of solidity and transparency,* as well as the specific compositional design elements of *geometry, movement, access, structure, concave and convex,* Seidler further illustrated successful architectural projects realized by modernist and contemporary architects. In the second instance, in the case of constructional logic, Seidler revisited the exemplary work of the Swiss engineer Robert Maillart (1872–1940) and the Italian engineer Pier Luigi Nervi (1891–1979), with whom Seidler collaborated in the design and construction of Australia Square (1961–67) and the MLC Centre (1971–77). Through them, he addressed the imaginative approach to structural problems and their interaction with architectural forms.

The synthesis of these two themes, with technology a counterpoint to art, can be read as the culmination of an *organizational design framework*. Sydney architecture historian Philip Drew proposed that such a design framework "reflects Seidler's foothold in modernism, and his belief in the synthesis of art and technology."[3] If we accept Drew's proposition, then Seidler's lectures express his belief that "the essence of modern architecture is based on a coherent ideology embracing and fusing visual and spatial imagination, technological integration and constructional logic."[4] New technologies and new materials introduced a freedom in the

3 Philip Drew, *Two Towers: Harry Seidler—Australia Square, M.L.C. Centre* (Sydney, 1980), p. 11.

4 "Harry Seidler Lectures on Architecture (1980)," lecture 1, "Interaction: Architecture and the Visual Arts," transcript, p. 3.

design and realization of certain buildings, because load-bearing walls were already obsolete by the end of the 1930s. For Seidler, designing continuous, dematerialized spaces created radical new possibilities. Thus, as the legacy of the modernist period, dematerialized spaces should be respected, re-evaluated, and relayed to students.

In terms of visual and spatial imagination, the first lecture, "Interaction: Architecture and the Visual Arts," clarifies Seidler's beliefs. It introduces students to the role and interaction of architecture with art. He explains, "The visual arts of our time have had as much to do with the visual language that has come to make up Modern Architecture." He further suggests, "The related community of principles aims and results in all the visual arts, evaluating the language of space, of visual tensions and generally showing what our eyes respond to positively, and just what the common denominators in our language of vision are today."[5] Seidler showed his students the exemplary work of cubist painters, and inter alia, the Bauhaus artists Joseph Albers (1888–1976), László Moholy-Nagy (1895–1946), and Johannes Itten (1888–1967), urging them to defy time and space by thinking in three dimensions.

In the second and fourth lectures, "Form Relations in Baroque and Modern Architecture," parts 1 and 2, Seidler revisits baroque architecture and asks his students to embrace creativity. He suggests "a survey of a significant period in history, which has been called the last great creative period prior to our own, illustrating and seeing the similarity of consequential thought, then and now, of system-geometry, spatial interplay and flair for dramatization."[6] Seidler mentions the Italian baroque architect Francesco Borromini and his church Sant'Ivo alla Sapienza and includes images of the building to illustrate the spatial imagination achieved through interior and exterior concave and convex forms that intertwine with each other in alternate bays and continue to the dome above. Seidler's words emphasize how its geometry and space lose the axial approach of the Renaissance period.

Seidler's belief that constructional logic underpins successful design is clarified in the third lecture, "Consequence of Design and Detail," which "sets the context for a vigorous student discussion on the impact of structure, material selection and construction technology on contemporary design principles and concepts. Seidler's ideas, resolutely tectonic in nature, formed the intellectual framework for the discussion."[7] Using examples from his own work, including the Thredbo Ski Lodge (1962), the Hong Kong Club (1980–84), and the Australian embassy in Paris (1973–77), he illustrates the organizational design framework, reinforcing the importance of a well-chosen structural theme and its impact on design decisions and material selection. For Alec Tzannes, "What was

5 Ibid., lecture 1, "Interaction: Architecture and the Visual Arts," transcript, p. 3.

6 Ibid., lecture 2, "Form Relations in Baroque and Modern Architecture, Part 1," transcript, p. 5.

7 Notes by Alec Tzannes for his introduction to lecture 3, presented at Lunch Time Lecture at the Faculty of the Built Environment, 4 September 2014, UNSW.

exemplary in Seidler's 'oeuvre' was evident. ... His design concepts were influenced by and sometimes led by the inevitable logic of structure, construction technique and material science. His was an architecture that integrated with deft skill and pragmatic realism advanced knowledge of contemporary design sciences, and technology and construction."[8] For example, Seidler's Trade Group Offices (later renamed the Edmund Barton Building), in Canberra, and the MLC Centre in Sydney were designed to use only three industrially produced concrete structural components: a long span beam that works also as a façade element (with continuous, recessed windows between them); a precast column; and a floor plank connected by pre-stressing wires to produce unity.[9] In the 2014 lecture and discussion, Tzannes made the point, "Ideas around the impact of contemporary construction techniques (that we felt would be embraced by Seidler if he were practicing today) included the use of advanced 'design-make' computational technology to continue his theme of 'pre-fabrication' to deliver innovative architectural form with economy."[10] In both the Trade Group Office and the MLC Centre, the constructional logic was a system of repetitive elements. In questioning what Seidler would do now, Tzannes suggested, "Today, the difference ... is that prefabrication using advanced computational technologies does not require the same level of repetition as in the Seidler era. Mass customization of building components is now available, creating more opportunity for the exploration of spatial and sculptural ideas that can be produced effectively and economically, in accordance with one of Seidler's dicta."[11]

Seidler's fifth lecture, "Habitat: Its Detail and Totality," observes the design of housing typologies in Australia and overseas. Seidler chides local architects for dismissing the lessons of modern architecture, stating, "I believe it is important to reiterate some of the creative origins, and where and what are the principles of modern architecture, where they have their roots and where are they going and, above all, where should we go."[12] Seidler designed housing typologies keeping in mind the lessons of the modernist period. Tzannes' discussion with students on Seidler's residential housing project, in particular the NSW Housing Commission Apartments as shown in the video of Seidler's Lecture 3, and its relation between spatial imagination and constructional logic explored the social impacts of innovative architecture when applied to social housing projects. This discussion included whether or not today's use of more familiar housing forms is a relevant factor for this building type, noting the responses by residents to Seidler's use of innovative construction techniques, and which included their feeling that they were 'experiments' for his design philosophies."[13]

8 Ibid.

9 "Harry Seidler Lectures on Architecture (1980)," lecture 3, "Consequence of Design and Detail," transcript, p. 5.

10 Notes by Tzannes for his introduction to lecture 3.

11 Ibid.

12 "Harry Seidler Lectures on Architecture (1980)," lecture 5, "Habitat: Its Detail and Totality," transcript, p. 2.

13 Notes by Tzannes for his introduction to lecture 3.

In his sixth lecture, "Principles in the Mainstream of Modern Architecture," Seidler asks the rhetorical question, "What, now, are the principles?" In response, he links spatial imagination and constructional logic, and how, for him, these two complementary aspects merge to realize the aesthetics of the modern architecture of the twentieth century. As a modernist architect, Seidler sought out successful artists, architects, and engineers for inspiration and collaboration, a point well made in lecture 6, when he suggests that what is called twentieth-century modern architecture is built upon "a synthesis of all the concerns of painters, sculptors, technicians, engineers."[14] Seidler speaks of this synthesis as "discernable criteria, which make up the principles of modern architecture recognizable in different ways in different parts of the word." In this lecture, he clarifies his belief in an architectural language that uses both influences from art and technology to foster creativity. In his own words, "The essence of modern architecture is based on a coherent ideology embracing and fusing visual and spatial imagination, technological integration and constructional logic."

It is possible that the themes from Seidler's lectures echo what might have been his first academic paper, published in Australia in October 1949. In "Painting toward Architecture," he strives for a world in which art and technology assist architecture to achieve a clear "dematerialization of space and mass." In Seidler's words, "We could simply say that aesthetically we want dematerialization, functionally we need it and technically we are free to bring it about."[15]

14 "Harry Seidler Lectures on Architecture (1980)," lecture 6, "Principles in the Mainstream of Modern Architecture," transcript, p. 5.

15 Harry Seidler, "Painting toward Architecture," *Architecture*, October 1949, p. 121.

16 Sigfried Giedion, *Space, Time and Architecture* (Cambridge, Mass., 1941).

Seidler's Milieu, 1940s–1980s

So, what did Seidler's themes from his 1949 "Painting toward Architecture" and 1980 Six Lectures have in common? One can find the answer in the formative influence of his architecture education and formal exposure to the Bauhaus pedagogy. From 1941 to 1944, Seidler attended the School of Architecture at the University of Manitoba, in Winnipeg, where he encountered the writing of Sigfried Giedion and its notion of space and time in art, architecture, and technology. Giedion's seminal book, *Space, Time and Architecture*,[16] introduced Seidler to the baroque connection to modernism, to the Bauhaus pedagogy of the U.S. émigrés Walter Gropius and Marcel Breuer, and to the ideas of technological framework as the basis of the design process of the Swiss engineer Robert Maillart.

The chapter "The Undulating Wall and the Flexible Ground Plan" begins with a celebration of Borromini's San Carlo alle Quattro Fontane, and Seidler's second lecture, in which he talks about the architectural inheritance of the baroque period, does so similarly. In Giedion's words, "Nowadays it is easy for us to see the force that appears in the whole structure, in the stressing of the progression and regression of the wall through the hollowing out of niches and the building up of contradistinguished parts. There is to be seen here a real molding of space, a swelling and receding that causes the light to leap over the front of the church."[17] Seidler remarks, "What happened in the Baroque time was a new concern and development of systems of geometry of a very, very high order and complexity. The two dimensionality of the Renaissance architecture is broken and of course that is an era that glorified the curve. A new power was found to mold space, almost to the point of portraying infinity."[18]

Invoking the technological and constructional abilities of Maillart, Seidler was influenced by Giedion's discussion on Maillart's innovative bridge designs, his own legacy of the modernist, which began by eliminating non-functional elements. Giedion wrote, "What Maillart has achieved is based on one idea: that is possible to reinforce a flat or curved concrete slab transforming that into an active bearing surface capable of assuming all forms of stress."[19] Consequently, the monumental heavy structure of a bridge with solid piers and beams is abandoned in favour of a more poetic and sinuous, curved structure lightly stretching over a river. Seidler showed examples, including the Schwandbachbrücke and the Salginatobelbrücke, both realized in Switzerland in 1933 and 1930, respectively.

As Seidler recognizes Giedion's responsibility for rediscovering the modernity of the baroque in his own time (1940),[20] Seidler himself can share responsibility for making available to the students in the graduation studio (1980) the historical continuum of the same baroque visual and structural principles. In the master's degree course in architecture at Harvard's Graduate School of Design (1945–46), Seidler discussed other aspects of the dematerialization of space and mass with Giedion, Gropius, and Breuer. Here, the Bauhaus diaspora found a receptive audience. So what does the Bauhaus tell us about Seidler's principles and who the main contributors were who emigrated from Germany?

The Bauhaus flourished in the United States following its initial formulation of art and crafts in 1919 Weimar that fused the arts, technology, painting, sculpture, and architecture into an inclusive combination of teaching and practice not only involving objects and buildings, but also large parts of a city. Studies in visual perception and abstract geometry were also translated into American architectural pedagogy at Black Mountain College,[21] where in 1946 Seidler took a course in material and design with Albers, another Bauhaus émigré.[22] Art and architecture historian Hanno-Walter Kruft, introducing the work of Gropius and the Bauhaus, wrote, "Gropius had a clear-cut view of the relationship between technology,

17 Ibid., p. 111.

18 "Harry Seidler Lectures on Architecture (1980)," lecture 2, transcript, p. 2.

19 Giedion, *Space, Time and Architecture*, p. 448.

20 "Harry Seidler Lectures on Architecture (1980)," lecture 2, transcript, p. 2.

21 Jeannine Fiedler and Peter Feierabend, eds., *Bauhaus* (Cologne, 1999), p. 63.

22 Vladimir Belogolovsky, *Harry Seidler: Lifework* (New York, 2014), p. 254.

design and aesthetics."[23] Gropius's architectural and structural innovations were explored in the Fagus-Werk (1911–13), one of his early works. In this project, one can see the design principles introduced first in Europe and later transported to Harvard: glass curtain walls, reinforced-concrete frames with cantilevered, floating floor slabs, thus his invention of the "dematerialized" corner, a strong influence in Seidler's future work in Australia.[24] Another Bauhaus émigré mentioned many times in Seidler's lectures, Moholy-Nagy, contributed to the architectural section at the Bauhaus with his view of space as "flowing spatial and articulated experiences."[25] Seidler interprets the concept of dematerialization of space and mass in terms of carving out a material in the same way the modernist sculptor Henry Moore (1898–1986) realized his sculptures. Indeed, Moore's abstract sculptures seem almost architectural in their relation between solid and void, a great example for enticing students to explore alternative ways of conceiving a building.[26] In his first lecture, Seidler remarks,

> Finally, the sculptor. The sculptor's language has always been one that has been most related to architecture. Henry Moore has for many years hollowed out his sculptures, which is a new vision compared to that of the past, which has tended to be the solid cube, the solid element surrounded by air. Here we have solidity penetrated by air and we are viewing the surroundings through the object itself, the dissolution, the dematerialisation of solidity that has occurred in the painter's world very much emphasised by the sculptor as well as the architect.[27]

For a modernist architect, the overall volume is opened up by the void of an interior courtyard or a double height space or an interior cantilevered floor slab, with the result that the space and mass of the building is dematerialized. As an example, Seidler points to Le Corbusier's Villa Savoye at Poissy, near Paris, "that is in fact *penetrated*; the eye looks right through this exterior space which is frozen and contained within the circumscribing rectilinear form of the building."[28]

Thus, Seidler's Six Lectures embody the essence of Bauhaus, taking the viewer back to the modernist period of the 1940s. Professor Barry Bergdoll wrote of Seidler's lecture 6,

> The lecture is really about the fact that there is a main stream that has never been broken. I think that is very much the vivid mindset of Harry Seidler here. He is the continuer of the modern movement. He is the inheritor, the carrier, in many ways the fulfiller of it. That conviction is very moving, but I

23 Hanno-Walter Kruft, *A History of Architectural Theory from Vitruvius to the Present* (London and New York, 1994), p. 370.

24 Stephen Sennott, ed., *Encyclopedia of Twentieth Century Architecture* (New York and London, 2004), p. 121.

25 "Harry Seidler Lectures on Architecture (1980)."

26 Ibid., lecture 6, transcript, p. 4.

27 Ibid., Seidler's lecture 1, transcript, p. 9.

28 Ibid., emphasis in original.

think it is interesting to point out, particularly for the students in the room, that you could almost have the impression that Harry Seidler had attended the Bahaus. He shows that as though this was the building of his own lifetime, but of course he was born right at the moment when, and that would have a great influence in his life, the Nazis were closing the Bauhaus school.[29]

Peter Blake remarks how Seidler's architecture stands out not only in Australia, but most important, in the world, "because he has refused to reject the lessons of his principal mentors—Walter Gropius and Marcel Breuer—as many others have for reasons which are questionable at best."[30] The lessons he learned as a loyal disciple, not only of Gropius and Breuer, but also of the other Bauhaus émigrés in the United States, can be seen in the planning composition of his numerous projects, beginning with the Rose Seidler House (1949) and his own house in Killara (1966). In Sydney, Seidler explored the dematerialization of space and mass, exploding the typical normal rooms of a house into a continuum of spaces, free-standing planes, and cantilevered floor slab. The constructional logic as organizational design framework is visible in both houses but using different construction techniques, as pointed out by Bergdoll: "But I think most historians would see the big shift there in the expression from this very light-weight engineering timber structure cantilevered off the ground [Rose Seidler House] to a structure with a great dependence on reinforced concrete [Killara House]."[31]

All can probably agree that by holding to the Bauhaus lessons and by challenging conventional contemporary design, Seidler nurtured in his students thought-provoking spatial and constructional investigations. In the same year of his appointment at UNSW, Seidler gave a talk at the Royal Australian Institute of Architecture entitled "Work in the Mainstream of Modern Architectural Development." Remarkably, his architectural thinking matches the Six Lectures in particular the last lecture 6 and reiterates the significance of Bauhaus émigré teaching and design work and their influence on the architectural language of current architecture. If 1980 is marked internationally by the theme of Paolo Portoghesi's Venice Architecture Biennale, "The Presence of the Past," and by postmodernist style, Seidler's 1980 lectures return to the Bauhaus and Giedion's *Space, Time and Architecture* with a respect for history and historical continuity.

29 Transcription by Paola Favaro of the recorded response of Barry Bergdoll to Seidler's lecture 6, Lunch Time Lecture, 18 September 2014, UNSW. Sincere thanks to Polly Seidler for providing the MP3 recording of Bergdoll's lecture and participating in the lecture.

30 Peter Blake, *Architecture for the New World: The Work of Harry Seidler* (Sydney, 1973), p. 7.

31 Bergdoll's response to lecture 6.

Asking, "What does it mean to bring back the Bauhaus?," Bergdoll proposed a plausible answer:

> So the Bauhaus had been eclipsed, and the modern architecture had been in a state of contestation before. Seidler's own training really comes from a second moment of what we might call the first transplantation of the notion of the Bauhaus. In fact, the Bauhaus is completely formed by the Bauhaus émigrés in the US, the Black Mountain College, where he encounters Albers, and Walter Gropius' Graduate School of Design and particularly his close friendship with one of his teachers, Marcel Breuer, that will continue as a life-long friendship.[32]

This historical continuity is visible in his lectures through the images of precedent and current architectural design. For example, images of Breuer's Whitney Museum (1963–66), in New York, with its visual solidity in a ziggurat form above a dematerialized glass wall, examples from Gropius, Le Corbusier, and Mies Van der Rohe, and examples from the contemporary clear geometry of I.M. Pei's East Wing of the National Gallery of Art, in Washington D.C., opened to the public in 1978, enrich his lectures and are clear indications of Seidler's continuity of modernist thought.

Adding weight to this argument, William Jordy notes how Seidler's architecture has been influenced by a "compact bundle of seminal influences" from his education at the Harvard Graduate School of Design, "where he received advanced architectural training under Walter Gropius and Marcel Breuer in 1946, ... to the contact with Oscar Niemeyer's architectural office and the professional collaboration with Pier Luigi Nervi." [33]

Jordy concludes his introduction arguing:

> Seidler's career demonstrates his life-long commitment both to the ideals and many of the formal themes of Modernism as these had evolved up to the decade after the Second World War. Undeflected from his early convictions by succeeding waves of Anti- and Post-Modernism, he has "stayed the course". Yet he has also steadily enlarged on his inheritance by structural, sculptural and geometric innovation, until his most recent buildings increasingly open to lyrical allusions.[34]

Jordy's words reinforce the argument of Seidler's full commitment to the themes of modernism in his architectural approach and practice. Notwithstanding, his approach to teaching architectural design in 1980 very much belongs to the modernist tradition of architectural inquiry taught in the

32 Ibid.

33 William Jordy, "The Migration of an Idea," in Kenneth Frampton and Philip Drew, *Harry Seidler: Four Decades, of Architecture* (London and New York, 1992), p. 11.

34 Jordy, "Migration of an Idea," p. 15.

same period at various schools in Europe and North America, where design was tested along with the formation of related theories. On a personal note, I can testify to a sympathetic congruence in the curriculum at the School of Venice in the 1980s, where the design studio with the architects and academics Carlo Aymonino (1926–2010) and Vittorio Gregotti (born 1927) was based on revisiting Le Corbusier's La Tourette monastery and other textbook modernist projects. Aymonino's *Il Significato della Citta'* (1975) and Gregotti's *Questioni di Architettura* (1986) made an important contribution to architectural theory looking back at the modern movement and at the same time looking forward to engaging with the complexity of the contemporary city. This engagement with the past, which in Seidler's eyes represented continuity from the modernist period and its possibilities of still being an answer to present design ideas was a theme that Seidler would eventually encounter and apply to his projects in Australian and European cities, including Canberra, Sydney, Paris, and Vienna.

1980 Studio: Student Projects

By 1980 Seidler had already designed and realized a large number of buildings, including a lauded series of houses in Sydney, Australia Square and the MLC Centre in Sydney's civic centre, and the Australian embassy in Paris. After 1980 the Sydney skyline would be enriched by Grosvenor Place (1982–88), Capita Centre (1984–89), Horizon Apartments (1990–98), and Cove Apartments (2003–04).

Arguably, in his lectures, as Bergdoll suggests, acting as the "professor" and invoking history to enhance students' creativity, Seidler prioritized modernist examples, the architecture of the baroque, and images from the Bauhaus artists and sculptors, deliberately leaving his own projects in the background or talking about them as they were part of the history of architecture. It is pertinent to revisit the work produced in 1980 by Seidler's students to discover the influence of his Six Lectures as well as signs of the planning organization and formal realization of his work. For example in the work of his student Mark Edward Butler, we read in the publication on the students' work,

> This project was considered one of the best in the group. It solved the diverse needs of a school of architecture in an almost "minimalist" painterly visual way. The whole complex is contained and circumscribed by a "hollowed out" square plan. The ordered simplicity of the scheme is evident in the consistent visual language used: the square, the quadrant and the diagonal. These occur and re-occur and are recalled in "counterpoints" throughout the composition.[35]

35 Jack, *Seidler Studio*, p. 8.

Here the influence of the Bauhaus artists is apparent, with the compelling images of Moholy-Nagy and Theo Van Doesburg, but so is Seidler's clear planning organization from his first statement the 1949 Rose Seidler House in North Sydney to the 1975 urban composition of the MLC Centre at Martin Place. As noted by Kenneth Frampton and displayed in the recent exhibition curated by Vladimir Belogolovsky,[36] Seidler's subsequent centre city developments like MLC Centre were treated as "cities in miniature."[37] This is probably the idea that characterizes Butler's work. His confident handling of the cubic form is enriched by a complexity of parts one would encounter in a city precinct but at the same time is "dematerialized" as in the examples shown by Seidler of Moore's sculptures. The mass is "hollowed out" to expose a framed courtyard both in plan and elevation visible in the images of the articulated model.

In Peter Kabaila's work, one sees the clear influence of Seidler's Thredbo Ski Lodge and its diagonal structural frame making a more visible connection with Seidler's theme of constructional logic. One is tempted to relate this student's design to Seidler's exploration of innovative structure combined with his deep understanding of the properties of materials as explored in lecture 3. Seidler's "euphoria for technology," as Bergdoll termed it in his lunchtime lecture, has influenced Kabaila's overall approach to a well-conceived design scheme. The publication on the students' work states,

> Two parallel wings with a long central space between them form the essence of this scheme. Uses not readily accommodated in the rectilinear forms of the wings, such as lecture rooms and hall, are housed in separate structures "pulled away" and connected. The structural design also employs both simple and direct ideas with some constructional acrobatics which, nevertheless, are plausible and sculpturally valuable. The repetition of the diagonal both horizontal and vertical in juxtaposition with the rectangle and quadrant, ties the composition together quite successfully.[38]

In contrast to this square and rectangular planning organization is the triangle form in the work of Greg Holman, whose work perhaps stands out not only for his acknowledgment of the 1920s–1940s modernist period and Seidler's work, but most important for embracing the 1980s contemporary work. The catalogue of student work reads,

> To attempt a combination of triangular and rectangular geometries in the same building is a brave act indeed. Very rarely, if at all, has this

36 Kenneth Frampton, introduction, in Belogolovsky, *Harry Seidler LifeWork*.

37 *Harry Seidler: Painting toward Architecture*, Museum of Sydney, November–March 2014, curated by Vladimir Belogolovsky and Caroline Butler-Bowdon.

38 Jack, *Seidler Studio*, p. 34.

> been done successfully in the history of modern architecture. I.M. Pei's museum in Washington restricts itself to triangular geometry exclusively and creates some superb effects. That well-known recent building probably stimulated this valiant effort.[39]

39 Ibid., 26.

40 Conversation with the architect Greg Holman, Harry Seidler & Associates, September 2014.

41 Seidler, "Painting toward Architecture."

According to Greg Holman, principal architect in 1980 for Harry Seidler & Associates, Seidler's Six Lectures "opened a new world to the students, broadening their visual and technological education."[40] Seidler's reference and homage to "painterly, sculptural and technological elements, which have reoccurred in architecture almost throughout the times,"[41] can be interpreted as the basis for an educated architectural imagination probably similar to the "total work of art" from the Bauhaus manifesto. As noted, the Bauhaus brought together art, technology, and architecture, and Seidler's Six Lectures have consistently explored the potential of the arts and technology to foster students' architecture creativity.

The 2014 Studio

Seidler's theoretical thinking for the 1980 architecture studio informed and served as the background for the third year architecture graduation studio in 2014 at UNSW, creating a train of thought for developing an educated imagination. Students' familiarity with the Six Lectures was important in contributing to the discussion and arguments raised by the three invited guests: Professor Xing Ruan, Architecture Programme director at the UNSW Built Environment who responded to Seidler's lec-ture 2, "Form Relations in Baroque and Modern Architecture"; UNSW Built Environment dean, Professor Alexander Tzannes, who introduced Seidler's lecture 3, "Consequence of Design and Detail"; and Professor Barry Bergdoll, professor of modern architectural history at Columbia University and curator in the Department of Architecture and Design at the Museum of Modern Art, who responded to Seidler's lecture 6, "Principles in the Mainstream of Modern Architecture."

Their points of view contributed to expanding the students' appreciation of certain aspects of architecture, questioning whether and how Harry Seidler's design principles from the Six Lectures are still relevant today, and arguably learning a structured "system of thinking" from the historical precedents presented—or in Seidler's words, "a coherent ideology embracing and fusing visual and spatial imagination, technological integration and constructional logic." Constructed in this way, the 2014 design studio was not only set up to explore design thinking, but to explore the way in which design thinking is generally shaped by theory and how theory in turn is shaped by prevailing attitudes and preoccupations. The academy is in a particular position to explore this relationship through the artful construction of pedagogical projects. Tzannes' notes relating to lecture 3 seem to suggest similar thinking:

> We concluded on the enduring value of understanding the integration of design concepts with material and construction knowledge as framed by Seidler's lecture. Advanced contemporary knowledge in these areas can inspire innovative design thinking, imaginative spatial arrangements and new visual language for architecture. Paraphrasing Seidler, sound design systems and principles were identified to underpin the design and construction of contemporary architecture, as relevant today as in Seidler's era.[42]

42 Notes by Tzannes for his introduction to lecture 3.

Conclusion

Based on examining Seidler's Six Lectures from 1980 and introducing them to a new cohort of students in 2014, this paper aimed to adopt Seidler's theoretical reflections on the Bauhaus lessons on visual education and spatial imagination, the geometrical enquiry of baroque compositions, and the structural innovations of Maillart and Nervi. By drawing directly on the lectures and brief devised by Seidler in 1980, students were introduced not only to his thought, but also to the world from which he came.

In his lectures, Seidler promoted the belief that the "essence of modern architecture is based on a coherent ideology embracing and fusing spatial imagination, technological integration and constructional logic." My own position, which underpins this "updating" of the Seidler studio, is that there is currently a lack in the realm of academics and among practitioners of such a coherent ideology. In this vacuum, project "decorations" accumulate, rather than signs of a clear and articulated system of principles. Drew ends *Two Towers* with an argument that substantiates this position. Referring to Australia Square and the MLC Centre, both designed before 1980, he wrote, "The towers embody important technical advances and demonstrate a skill in handling form, which is only possible where the architect is clear in his own mind about the proper tasks of architecture."[43]

43 Drew, *Two Towers*, p. 11.

The argument that Seidler's controversial public statements against postmodernism have restrained Sydney architects from fully embracing postmodernism is plausible. It is widely accepted that his architecture has affected the tone of the civic centre of Sydney in a positive sense. Visiting Seidler's city towers, and passing through their expressive external volumes into their animated interior spaces, one experiences what Seidler advocated in his 1964 article "Architecture Appropriate to Australia": "Planes opposing each other in space … solid opposed by void, cold colour against warm, curve against straight line and above all in Australia's climate, sunlight against shadow."[44]

A big difference between 1964 and today in general culture is the increased saturation of media, posing the risk of a derivative, imitative culture that does not develop an intellectual and informed generation of architecture students. Vladimir Belogolovsky suggests in his recent publication *Harry Seidler LifeWork*,

> Today architects and students all over the world dig through the latest publications and visit the newest buildings in search for new design ideas. The work of Harry Seidler directs them to find inspiration in many original sources and to explore numerous possibilities in their interpretations to address their own time and place.[45]

From the vantage point of the present, which seems to privilege what has been ironically called decorated sheds, how might one still understand, appreciate, and learn from Seidler's Six Lectures the *potential* of the modernist period, enthusing students with the principles of modern architecture? The following proposition by Seidler, from lecture 1, seems to respond to this question:

> To sum up, I would say that these tendencies shown are not necessarily evident to most people. People tend to not want formulas, not want to recognise criteria that should guide us, but in my view unless there are criteria, unless there is consensus about that which does influence and tantalize the eye in our age, it would be very difficult for us to find and explore those directions that have proven, at least for half, if not three quarters, of a century to be considered beautiful, satisfying and worthy of pursuit into the future.[46]

Thus, with these words, encouraging both a step toward the past and a vision toward the future, one can only hope that Seidler's Six Lectures will be influential to architecture students in the near future. By borrowing from the Italian writer Italo Calvino's *Lezioni Americane: Sei proposte per il prossimo millennio* (American lessons: Six proposals for the next millennium), a book based on Calvino's six lectures written in the early 1980s for the Charles Eliot Norton lectures at Harvard, Seidler's Six Lectures might be re-named "Australian Lessons: Six Proposals for the Next Millennium."

44 Harry Seidler, "Architecture Appropriate to Australia," *Architecture Today*, August 1964, p. 15.

45 Belogolovsky, *Harry Seidler: Lifework*, p. 11.

46 "Harry Seidler Lectures on Architecture (1980)," lecture 1, p. 9.

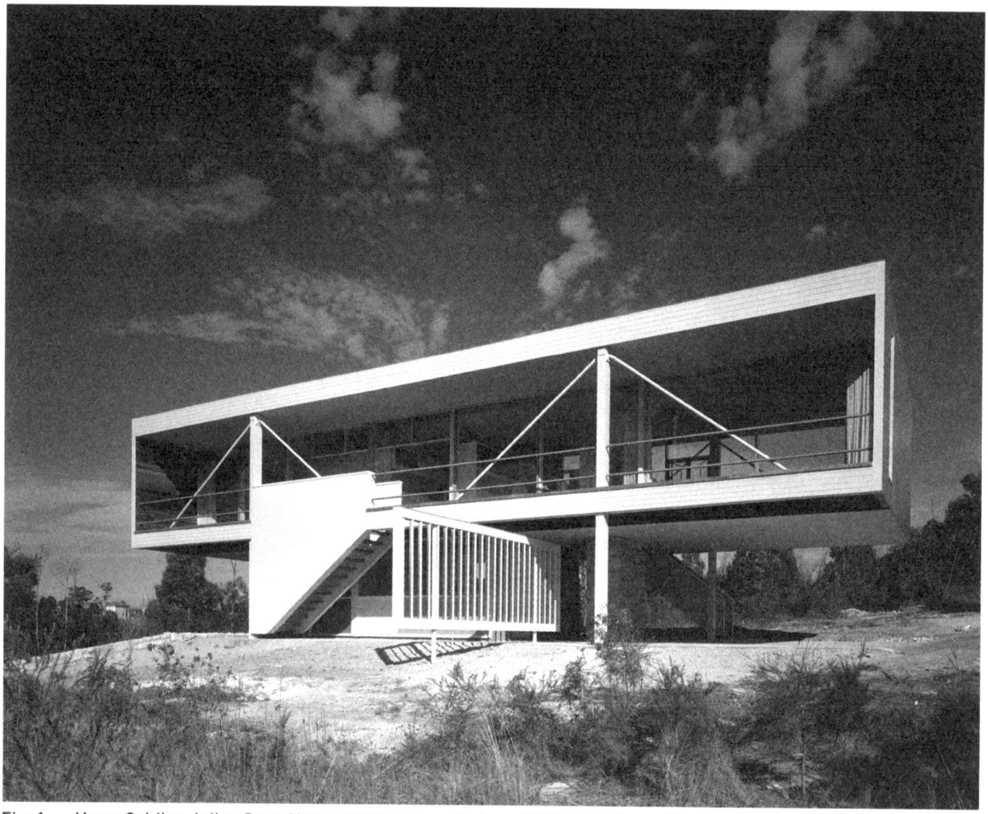

Fig. 1 Harry Seidler, *Julian Rose House*, Wahroonga, Sydney, 1949–54, Photo: Max Dupain, 1954.

HARRY SEIDLER AND REDUCTIVE ART IN AUSTRALIA

Billy Gruner

Harry Seidler once said, "There is a great misconception that modernism is a style. It isn't. It is a methodology of approach in constant flux, constant change."[1] With projects dating back to the mid-century comprised of superb dwellings, iconic skyscrapers, and much in between, Seidler's restatement of "purist" styling has been well documented, but there are matters to uncover beyond connections to Bauhaus modelling.[2] The extensive use of a "modern" language or set of evolving encoded principles proved a foundation for Seidler's success and explains why current Australian post-formalist artists familiar with this language regard the reductive art found in Seidler's projects inspiring and contemporaneous.[3]

Curating Seidler City

Seidler's architectural imprint on Sydney and its stunning cityscape is impressive. It is for this reason that Sydney has been referred to as Seidler City. Looking through the windows of Seidler's architecture, one sees an archiving of modern Australian art dating back to 1948. Seidler and his architect partner and wife, Penelope, created a stark and beautiful architectural legacy. Working alone or later with a committed team of associates, their projects and grounds were austerely fitted out via a stringent cogency of design (see, for example, Fig. 1). The detailed furnishings alongside significant local and international contemporary art pieces were thoughtfully selected.

The artworks they chose evolved thematically within a frame of criticality and panache, and today, without question, this forms a type of curated oeuvre, as evidenced throughout Max Dupian's photo archives. Importantly, it should be noted that Seidler rejected the term *international style,*[4] preferring that others simply consider his work as evolving.[5] This was a notion he learned from the Bauhaus master Walter Gropius, who encouraged a pre-emptiveness in Seidler's thinking in the 1940s. This influenced Seidler's early curatorial vision toward the broader acquisition of specific styles of contemporary art for his Australian projects.[6] Notably, the 1960s and 1970s in Sydney were a time when few outside of museum teams were actively curating radical contemporary art collections. Moreover the larger public artworks Seidler admired always spoke of planar transparency and a reorganized view of cubist space, with works by Alexander Calder, Charles O. Perry, Morris Louis, Frank Stella, Sol LeWitt, and Robert Owen underscoring then-lesser-known but no-less-significant local artworks.[7] In brief, the Seidlers' efforts over many decades bear witness to a genuine culturally responsive rigour throughout.

What compounds this impression of curatorial integrity is that many of the international reductive artworks chosen for projects were identified during visits to artists' studios. Such was the case with Frank Stella's *Pillars and Cones* (1984–87), selected from a black and white maquette seen during a studio visit in 1983 and later shipped to Australia for the Grosvenor Place project (Fig. 2). These unusual works of Stella's, in my opinion, add a postmodern sensibility to the project.[8] By using archival photographers like Max Dupain and others, a commitment to artistic process, extending from plan drawings to site completion, today offers a longer-term view of these works as a form of public "art collection."[9] This approach amounted to a cultural gift for clients as much as a public benefit, with few clients making changes to the art and décor or making unnecessary additions.

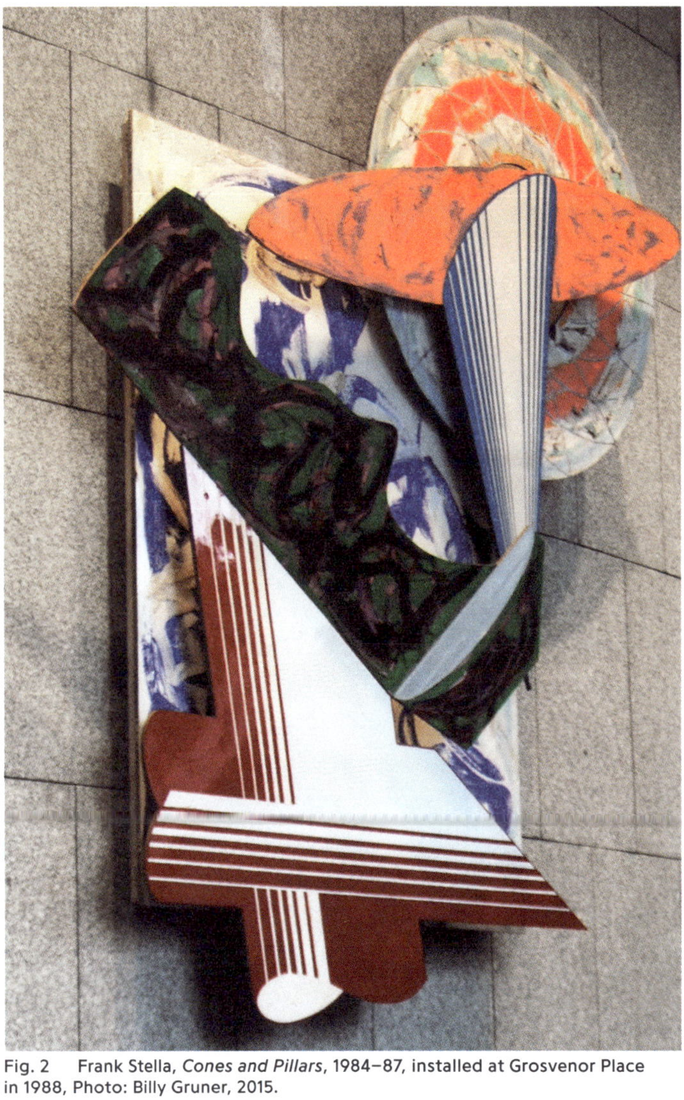

Fig. 2 Frank Stella, *Cones and Pillars*, 1984–87, installed at Grosvenor Place in 1988, Photo: Billy Gruner, 2015.

Curiously there is a regional myth that Seidler only sought out international artists for his projects, but this is not the case. The content by celebrated Australian abstractionists, Antipodean-style figurative artists, and indigenous artists that formed the body of curated works for his projects is far broader than perceived. In fact, Seidler was heavily involved with the Contemporary Art Society when he first arrived in Australia, and he personally paid for a large quantity of Australian artworks of all styles to be shipped from a government-owned collection for the opening of his Australian embassy in Paris in the 1970s. Seidler thought it essential that Aboriginal art be represented in the Paris embassy.

This alone illustrates his personal commitment to broader cultural support than previously credited,[10] and it was done at a point in time before the global impact of indigenous art on the international market was manifest. The National Gallery of Australia collection in Canberra did not have any such works available, so Seidler personally donated a large Aboriginal bark painting, *Kinga, The Legendary Crocodile* (artist unknown), from the Oenpelli area of Arnhem Land.[11] After media coverage of Seidler's donation and the lack of available art, the Australia Council agreed to permanently lend some Aboriginal works, including five Western Desert canvases, five Western Desert canvas boards, six bark paintings, a bone box, two Tiwi figures, and two burial poles. The Dupain photographs below show the two burial poles in the multipurpose hall of the Paris embassy (with the Eiffel Tower in the background) and the embassy apartments with one of the Aboriginal artworks (Figs. 3 and 4).[12]

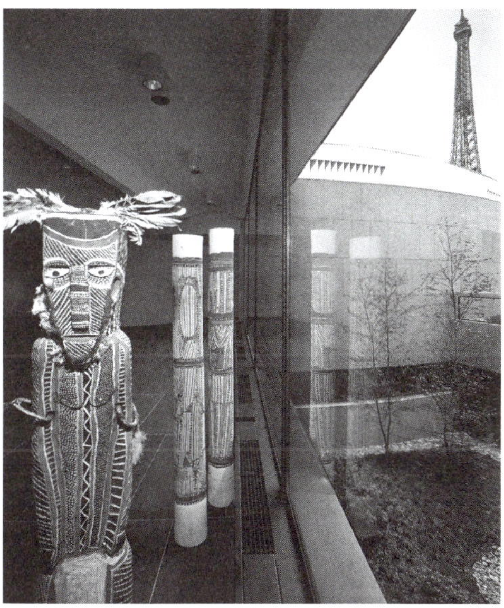

Fig. 3 *Tiwi poles*, Australian, Paris, embassy, multi-purpose hall, Photo: Max Dupain, 1978.

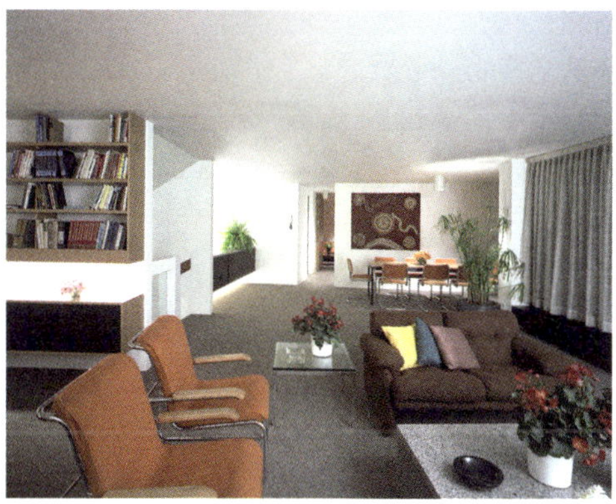

Fig 4. *Australian embassy apartment*, Paris, with a listed Aboriginal painting, artist unknown, Photo: Max Dupain, 1978.

The Seidlers' independent approach was a unique critical intervention that from any curator's purview would appear a considered experimentation in taste, style, and boundaries within a regional context. Based only on a select few of the Australian works in situ, the Seidlers' conviction and decisive approach in curation nevertheless stirred critical opinion over stylistic preferences in Australia. Actually, the debate over the signature conflation of figuratively abstract and hard-core abstraction in the Seidler projects often flagged a social demand. The Seidlers' early mixing of visual codes sparked debate over the socio-political implications of art in public places. Irrespectively, the surety they expressed affected local art historicism and contemporary reductive art circles.[13]

The Primary 1950s: Dwelling in Red Yellow Blue White and Grey

Born in Vienna and fleeing early on from the looming troubles of war, Harry Seidler undertook a difficult journey, traveling to England sometime after his brother's arrival there. Their internment by the British landed both of them in Canada.[14] He later traveled on his own to the United States, where he was awarded a scholarship to study at Harvard, where he would learn from the Bauhaus masters Walter Gropius and Marcel Breuer.[15] The Seidler family, dislodged and separated during the war years, would later reunite and immigrate to Australia.[16] Seidler, however, stayed behind in the United States, receiving inspirational training from Josef Albers at Black Mountain College.[17] It was there that Seidler took the famous colour theory course.[18] Following this, Seidler worked with Breuer in his newly established private practice in New York, producing classic dwellings that made both of their modern styling valued as icons of advanced domestic dwelling. They demonstrably defined the innovative mid-century binuclear look.[19] He received additional input from Oscar Niemeyer, whose radical organic thinking was also admired.[20]

Seidler's activity in the early days of the late 1940s and 1950s in Sydney are poignant given that soon after arriving, the architect began winning awards for his Red Yellow Blue White and Grey dwellings (see Fig. 5). These houses influenced numerous Australian artists, designers, architects, and others. The Australian artist John Nixon introduced me to a range of the early, colourful houses in the 1990s.[21] As a key figure in Australian reductive art, he then emphasized to me that Seidler's work was invaluable to regional reductive art and architectural history, especially in relation to an extensive network of contemporary visual art groups engaging reductive language. The important regional circles today are Sydney Non Objective (SNO),[22] on Australia's east coast, and the Australian Centre for Concrete Art (AC4CA),[23] on the West coast, and many others in an international network of project spaces. They represent groupings of educated artists retracing and sharing information. What's understood is the value of select lineages, including Seidler. What is known is that radical coding or historic stylistic interests reappear in language via homage. A Seidler connection is appreciated by Australian reductive art makers and architects in turn.

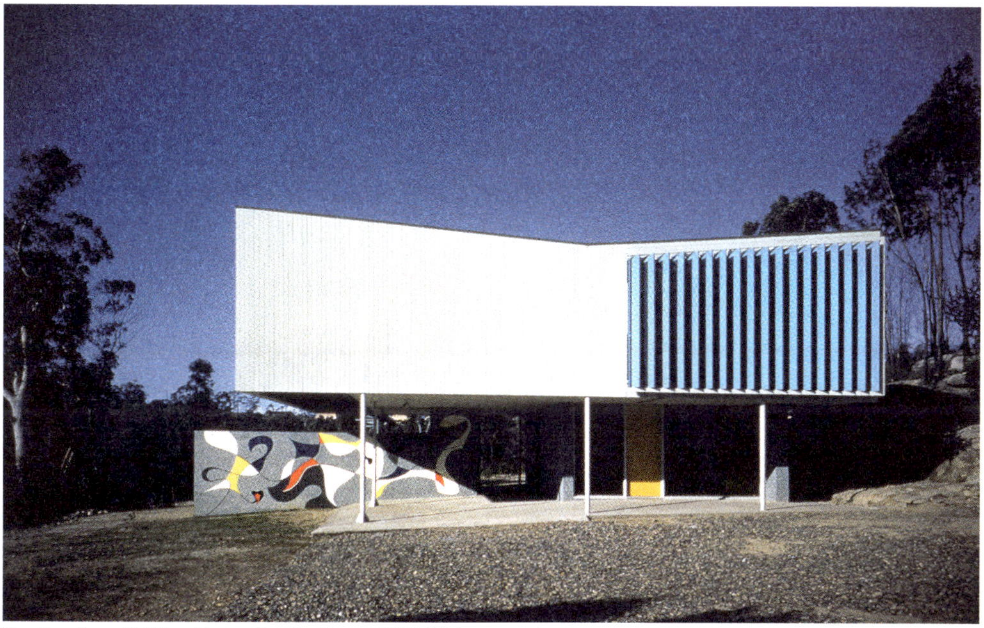

Fig. 5 Harry Seidler, *Marcus Seidler House*, 1953, Wahroonga, Sydney. Building and mural by Harry Seidler, Photo: Marcell Seidler, 1953.

Modernism Is Not a Style

Harry Seidler belongs to a long list of significant modern regional architects, including Harold Desbrowe-Annear, Robyn Boyd, the Burley-Griffins,Horbury Hunt, Richard Leplastrier, Bill Lucas, Glen Murcutt, and Ken Woolley, to mention a few.[24] In Seidler's 1949 paper "Painting toward Architecture," he noted, "There is a tendency today, even amongst architects themselves, to over-stress the significance of functionalism."[25] Seidler regularly said, "Modernism is not a style," implying he felt the notion of modernism had problems and was unnecessarily narrowing, a point he would belabour his whole life.[26] In a TV interview with the Australian Broadcasting Corporation, Seidler discussed the way modernism was perceived, citing Gropius, who alerted students to the cliché use of terms like *international style* and *modernism*. He stated,

> What he [Gropius] made me understand was that there is nothing new, really, that architecture in the past has always been an amalgam of the tastes

> of the time, the technology of the time. Gropius was a great advocator about which direction architectural design and industrial design should take. What people build is always an amalgam of their taste and their technological means. ... That's why I think it's a great misnomer to talk about a "modern" style. Style is a fixed set of rules about the way things look, whereas I think there's a continuum of constant change because what the eye requires or demands will come forth through the artists of the time. ... Gropius was one that made this clear to us, and I think it is *impossible* to argue against that.[27]

This points to the issue of how the currency of Seidler's architectural legacy should be appreciated, if not held within a considered relationship to contemporary art concerns. For example, Seidler's interest in transparent planes, arc, and segment construction of form was inspired by the works of two American sculptors: Charles O. Perry and Norman Carlberg. They shared a language that informed his own practice. Vladimir Belogolovsky recently suggested that what may be missing from our perceptions of Seidler's influence was a powerful relationship to reductive art. He variously discusses how Seidler's working of a reductive code was championed throughout this career.[28] I concur, seeing this as a specific annotation to a practice carrying considerably broader cultural value beyond architectural matters. What is implied is that Seidler's entire contribution to the regional art and architectural legacy may not be a given. If, however, one considers Seidler's systemic use of modern language via an appreciation of artistic systems, his complex methodology was as graphically based as conceptually and artistically valid.

Homage:
Through the Window of Architecture
We See Art

As noted, Seidler found himself in Sydney in the 1950s, far from the major centres like New York or London. Even in this then-remote location, he contributed toward a significant and emergent culture during the mid-twentieth century. There is no doubt he participated in the unfolding of an "alternate" modern history with many still-pending art and architectural outcomes to be researched. Overall, what matters is that he produced an artistic interpretation using his own voice, a variation or difference expressed within modernist mainstays made tangible via a specific regional production. More broadly, Australia and New Zealand, situated at a tyranny of distance, so to speak, have nonetheless generated an ongoing art-critical traction, their own cultural flavour within so-called modernist discourse. Discussion on that form of contemporary discourse simultaneously attends to a postcolonial arena of theoretic criticisms.[29]

In brief, peering through the windows of Seidler's major architectural works, one first sees the commissioned contemporary art, but through fresh readings what should be proffered is a more fitting evaluation of regionally specific, twentieth-century art and architecture concerns (Figs. 6 and 7). The question is, What may be implied in terms of Seidler's choices or homage to local art makers, especially given that many of the works the Seidlers' chose were by artists seeking to highlight ideas made in response to late twentieth-century demands, pressures, and new styles? A form of regional aesthetic or responsive generic approach opens out upon closer examination.

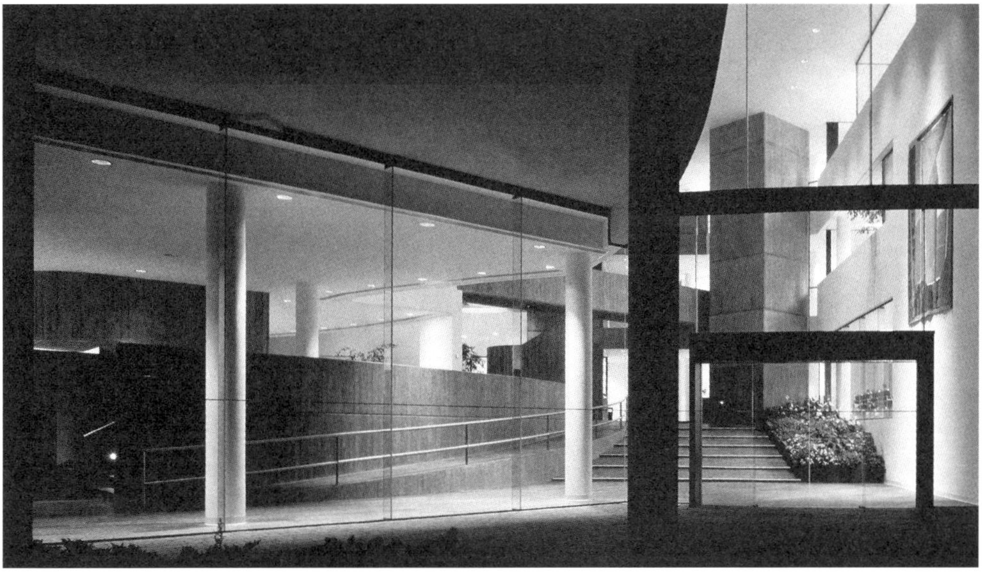

Fig. 6 Michael Johnson, *Ambroglio*, 1983, tapestry on the right wall at Waverly Civic Centre, now City of Monash, Melbourne, Photo: John Gollings, 1985.

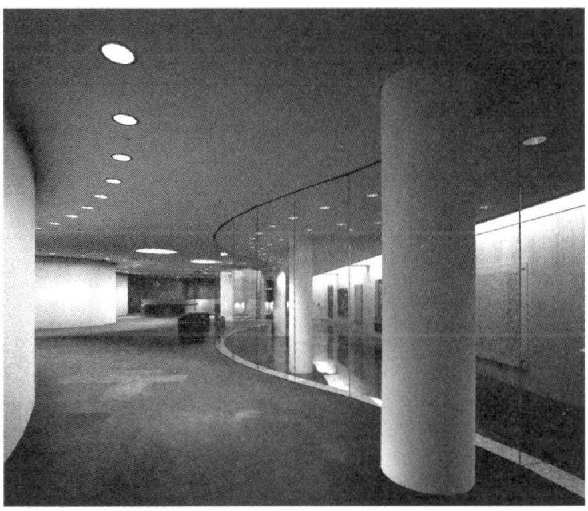

Fig. 7 *Shell House Gallery*, now 1 Spring Street, Melbourne, Photo: John Gollings, 1985.

The above distinctive modernist works by regional artists illustrate a point just mentioned but also allude to the notion of homage in late twentieth-century art, and when discussing Seidler, the matter of homage looms large. The many local art makers recommended to clients—for instance, Frank Hodgkinson, Peter Upward, John Olsen, John Coburn, Sydney Ball, David Aspden, Ron Roberson-Swann and Hilarie Mais had defrayed responsive practices for public scrutiny into their high-profile projects. Seidler's avant embassy project in Paris had artworks by Aspden, Ball, and Gunter Christmann, to mention a few of the Australians whose pieces he selected to be loaned from the collection of the National Gallery of Australia in Canberra.[30] It is reasonable to claim that the exotic modern outcomes produced by the Australians Seidler admired made clever, productive, and individualized use of the tool of homage to generate new work, albeit mostly within the genre of pure abstraction. Mais's sculptural object works are a case in point (Fig. 8).

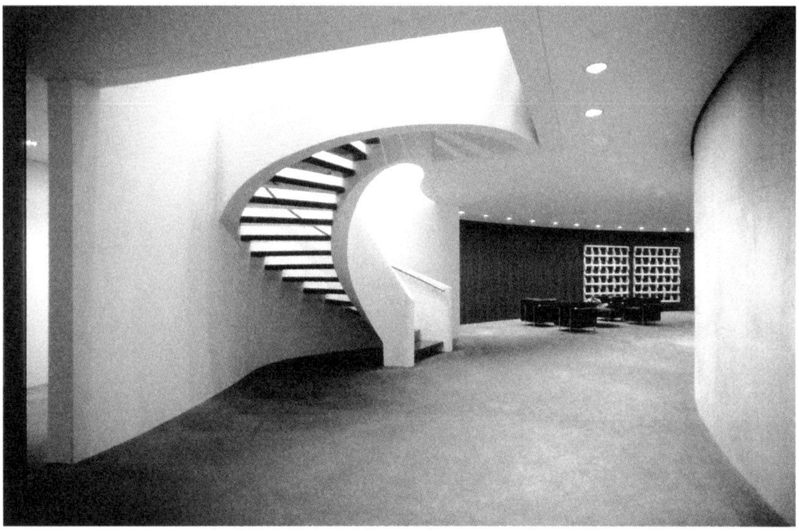

Fig. 8 Hilarie Mais, *Spectre*, 1989, Shell House, Melbourne, Photo: Harry Seidler, 2014.

In looking back over the postmodern era's favouring of an "anything goes" principle,[31] or more direct and less critical styles of appropriation that Seidler distrusted, the topic of intent within homage has real currency.[32] What is reasonable to assert is that Seidler illustrated over many decades an exemplary lesson through a refined vernacular of shared, coded languages in modern architecture and art defrayed. The reductive language embraced by the Seidlers, despite phasing in and out of valency over time academically, when it was combined with an astute sense and utilization of appropriate conceptual ideas, must be seen as central to any generalized discussion of Seidler's art-critical significance overall.

Interrelationship in Post-Genres and Figurational Bias

Seidler's life work marks a remarkable provenance in reductive practices and related contemporary art/architectural interests in Australia. To support this opinion, it is necessary to point to an area in which I have played a role. After graduating from the University of Sydney, a school based on the Bauhaus model of education, I engaged in work defined by government agencies as "emergent artists practices" at SNO. This is mentioned because there are some select artists who worked under commission with the Seidlers who were later curated in SNO projects, reinforcing stylistic preferences expressed about the Seidlers' production over many decades. I believe the much later curatorial work done at SNO in the area of abstraction and concrete art further attests to what Belogolovsky's exhibition writing explores and what John Nixon suggested much earlier—that the Seidler legacy represents an invaluable set of situations, commissions, and specific engagements with artists.[33] One key Australian artist shown was Robert Owen. Seidler saw Owen's work at the Art Gallery of NSW in 2004 and found that they shared some values and interests. This resulted in Owen being awarded a commission in 2006 to supply works for Seidler's MLC Centre in Sydney.[34] The work, *Interlude–Double Weave,* pays direct homage to Albers (Fig. 9). Importantly, as a pure abstractionist piece, it is also a discursive work asserting a visual relationship to social narratives, first, with respect to the female weavers of the Bauhaus, and second, in its green and purple end bars, the colours adopted by the early suffragettes in Australia.

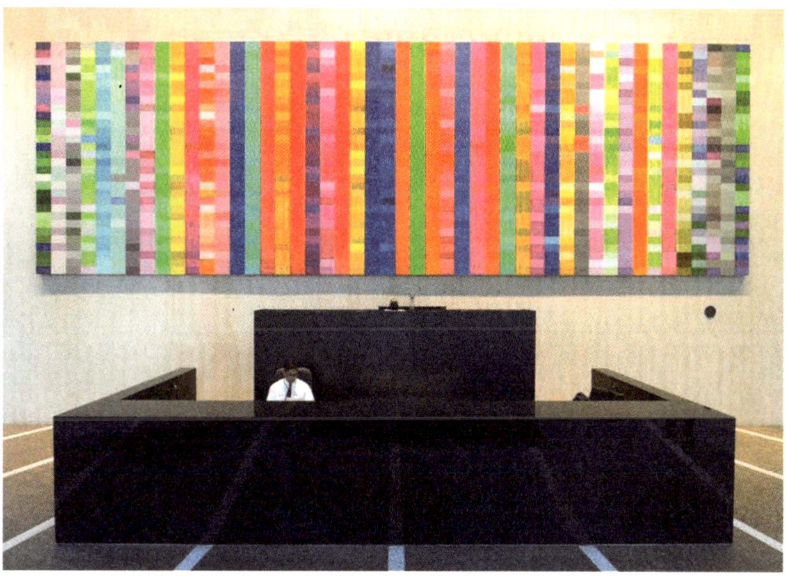

Fig. 9 Robert Owen, *Interlude – Double Weave*, 2006–07, MLC Centre, Sydney, Photo: John Marmaras, 2008.

Interlude–Double Weave can be seen by all who pass by the massive foyer windows of the MLC Centre, but as Owen states, "Visually encoded cues take the eye to the windows, to opacity, outside, to nature and the world."[35] The work, despite stating its non-objective credentials, is a meta-narrative located in relational histories. Its architectural setting, however, remains tantamount by authorial intent. It is also pure art with no enforced meaning. With that stated, what was most apparent from personal engagement with specialized emergent practices like Owen's and Ball's conducted over the last decade was the clear and unequivocal fact that there had been a significant arrival or language-specific movement in contemporary art taking place, and the Seidlers openly engaged with that. Owen iterated,

> While a student at the National Art School, we were taken to see [the] Rose Seidler House. That literally stunned me, and I loved the mural. I then travelled from 1963 to '75 overseas and worked with the British constructivist movement. Importantly, I first met Harry and Penelope properly later in 1986. Eric Orr from [the] Light and Space group in California was staying with me, and I installed Orr's work for the Seidlers at their own home after it was exhibited in the Biennale of 1986. Harry's influence had long been in the background of my thoughts, and at my survey exhibition at the AGNSW [Art Gallery of NSW] in 2004 he gave a genuinely felt sense of knowing, that he knew my work … and conveyed the idea of Naum Gabo's, that abstraction actually arises from a place deep inside, from a singular source … and Harry was in tune with this. Unfortunately he had a debilitating stroke six months later … and we didn't get to speak again.[36]

The SNO programme, getting under way in the early 2000s, had from the beginning been affiliated with young and senior artists of a high academic calibre, yet it was generally considered unauthorized as a culturally relevant project.[37] Nevertheless, it focused toward and connected to like-minded projects abroad, such as the Center for Contemporary Non-Objective Art (CCNOA) in Brussels,[38] PS in Amsterdam,[39] Minus Space in New York,[40] ParisCONCRETE, and Non-Objectif Sud (NOS) in the south of France.[41] In affiliating with other projects interested in reductive art, SNO shared the view that it is a genre best understood in relationship to other legacies born out of alternate formations of modern history.[42] Put another way, the projects were characterized by the shared belief that reductive art was not and remains separate from "abstract" art, the iconic other end of figurative art. New and responsive work was, as Seidler might say, just modern. This matter Owen also relationally discussed:

> To understand Harry Seidler's informing work, you need to get into the core of things. Harry produced extraordinary results that way. His was an educational role in helping Australians understand modern architecture. The Josef Albers mural inspired [MLC Centre] and helped me understand internationalist influence is fragmented, unlike in Europe, where it was continuous. Postmodernism tried to throw the baby out with the bath water concerning the Bauhaus, ... [which] had always tried to be inclusive and not just minimal or narrow in view. An interrelationship of art, music, and architecture was an important part of being a whole person, artist, especially when working with the influence of legacy in contemporary terms. Harry Seidler is a role model for that ideal. He was criticized for lack of inclusion of Australian artists, yet he presented many and brought others in long before biennale teams realized the term "international" could be used to defeat parochial forces. But he didn't dumb down his choices or choose those who wouldn't rise to the occasion. ... I felt Harry worked with his own drive and raised it all to the best he could possibly achieve.[43]

Owen went on to say, "In retrospect to provincialism issues, Harry Seidler brought intellect to local tastes."[44] There is evidence of a new interest in Seidler's aesthetic in the conflagration of productions that have been issuing forth worldwide from an array of specialist reductive art spaces since around 2000. Most important, by adopting figures from their own histories (regional or central), icons like Seidler are being re-valued in local histories as key providers and profoundly influential. In that system, prior readings of Australian visual arts and culture, for example, are being radically repositioned. In Seidler's case, the legacy of coded developmental practices has possibly never been more relevant to fans of art than it is now.

Contemporary reductive artists, designers, musicians, and architects are often characterized by a common refusal to be defined as minimal, as this is understood as paying narrow respect that seemingly ignores an earlier European history of "art concrete" art makers beholden to a history dating to Theo Van Doesburg and the De Stijl movement in the 1930s and back to Malevich and the constructivists.[45] Older figurationist-inspired terms like *abstract art* are dropped altogether within a refreshed process of critical engagements.

A new wave of "modern" makers are simply seeking clarity of meaning within artistic intent in the present. In short, new language is required to discuss current work fittingly, a demand since the late 1990s.

Post-formalist research shows this is now a heavily occupied zone comprising contemporary reductive artists of all kinds.[46] Therefore, a certain idealism is restaked. That is a fitting approach to homage combined with the calculated defrayment of constructive development activity of new makers seems to be a simple strategy to pursue, once it has been staked out.

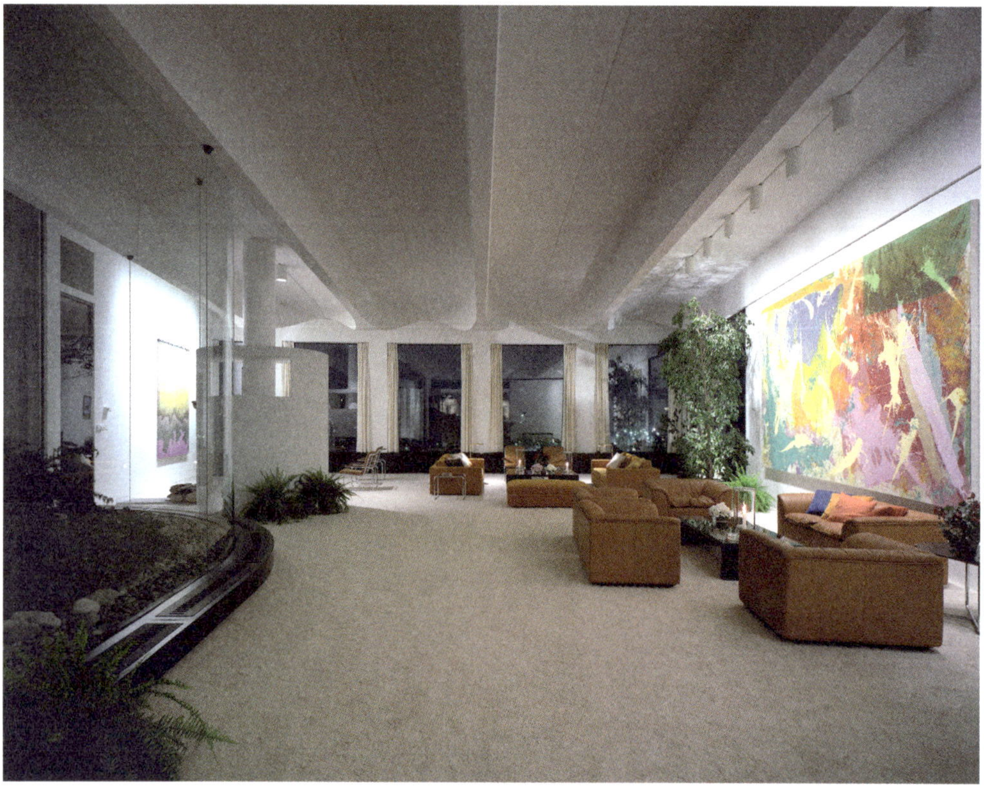

Fig. 10 Sydney Ball, *Heriot Wall*, 1973 (here upsidedown), Australian embassy, Paris; artwork on the left: Gunter Christmann *Brightscape*, 1972, Photo: Max Dupain, 1978.

Harry Seidler and New Idealism

The Seidler legacy is a unique architectural intervention in Australia's art and cultural life. What is seen in its purview recalls the drama of modernism, yet Seidler's cityscape also represents a masterful changing of public taste. It is, moreover, a challenging of morays and traditions that began before and climaxed at the height of a postmodern re-contextualization of art and architectural debate.[47] This has seen architects like Frank Gehry, Zaha Hadid, Kazuyo Sejima, and Gae Aulenti taking off in other expressively interpretive directions.[48]

Having the pioneering Italian structural engineer Pier Luigi Nervi assist with Australia Square was a visionary move forty years ago.[49] Seidler took a modern style appreciated by a few select clients and forged it into a form of critical city planning transgression, a tasking of academic morays, a challenge to rule and regulation, and defiance of outmoded codes in major projects. The MLC Centre showed a super-charged passion for an overall integrity of design sensibility and quality defrayment of contemporary art to augment it. As noted, the Australian embassy in Paris featured the large colour paintings of Christmann and Aspden plus a massive Ball *Stain* painting and a treasure trove of other works borrowed from the National Gallery of Australia collection in Canberra (Figs. 10 and 11). It is an international example of radical work of equally high calibre. The result for satisfied clients was quality to be proud of decades after intellectual fashions had changed.

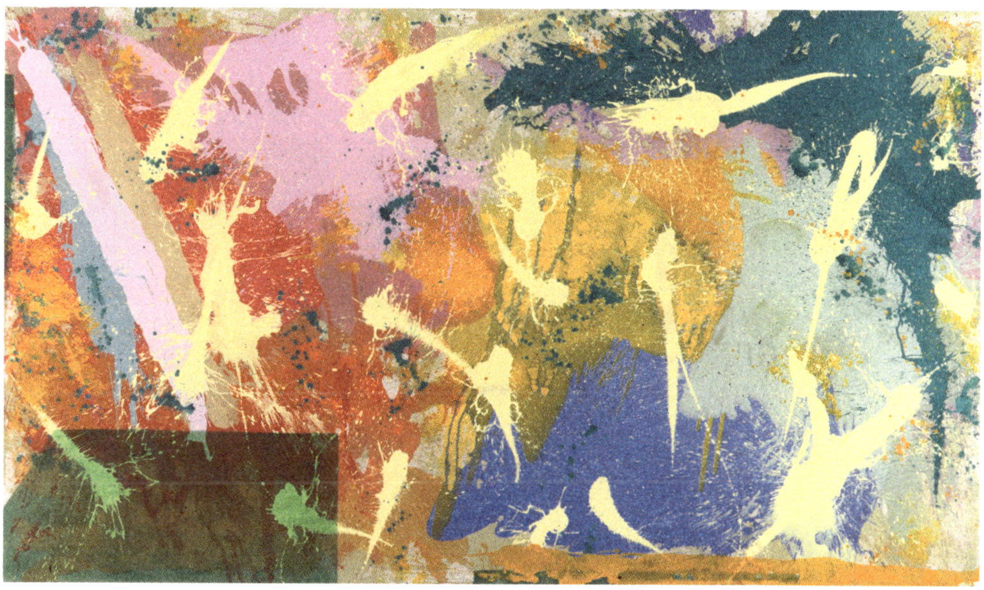

Fig. 11 Sydney Ball, *Heriot Wall*, 1973 (detail).

These projects highlight that Harry and Penelope Seidler were connected to many Australian artists (Figs. 12 and 13). Peter Hirst, the principal associate for Seidler & Associates for more than fifty years, Harry's daughter Polly, and Penelope all confirmed this in recent conversations. Such artists included John Olsen, John Coburn, Frank Hodgkinson, Peter Upward, Emanuel Raft, and Clement Meadmore (all of whose work appeared in Seidler designs from the 1950s and 1960s), Gunter Christmann (1970s), Sydney Ball (1970s and 1980s), and Ron Robertson-Swann, John Firth-Smith, Michael Johnnson, and Hilarie Mais (1980s). Among other artists included in projects by the Seidlers were David Aspden (1970s and 1980s) and Mandy Martin and Jenny Watson (1980s).[50] What matters is they all added to a vernacular producing inherent identifying detail, a new Australian-ness. The deconstructive and feminist-inspired work of Mais in the Shell House, Melbourne, is another example of the radical and reductive contemporary art the Seidlers acquired.

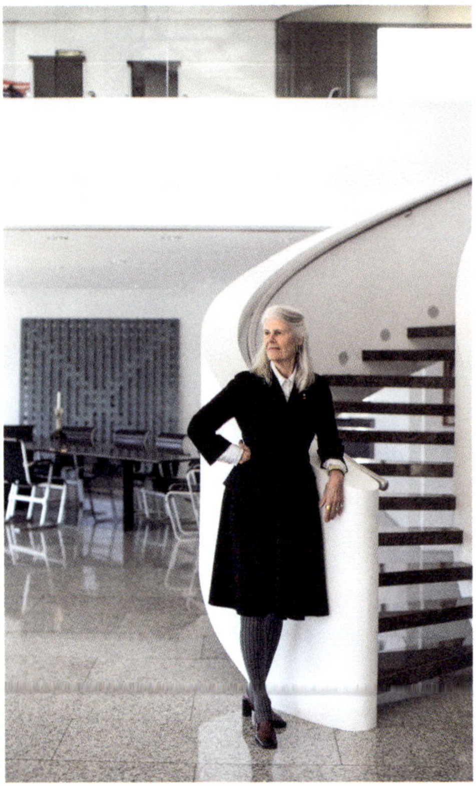

Fig. 12 Penelope Seidler at the Seidler Penthouse, Milsons Point, New South Wales, 2014. In the background is Hilarie Mais, *Gaea*, 1988, commissioned by Harry Seidler for Penelope Seidler's fiftieth birthday, Photo: James Horan, date unknow.

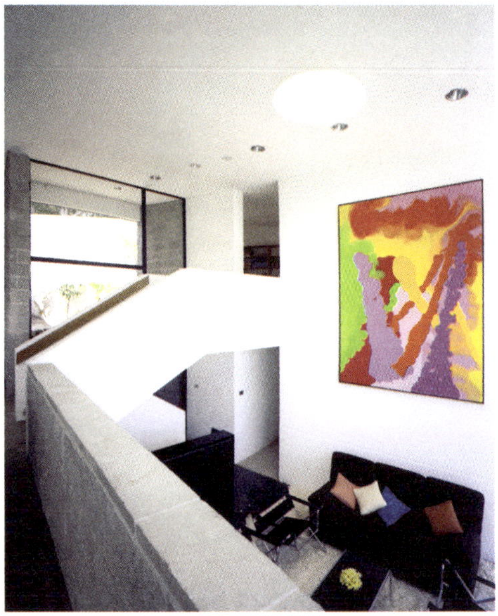

Fig. 13 *Merson House*, Palm Beach, New South Wales, with a work by Ron Robertson-Swann, Photo: Max Dupain, 1983.

During a visit to Seidler & Associates, Penelope was asked whether she felt she and her husband had had a fitting engagement with Australian art? She responded, "Of course we did."[51] Given that the interview was filled with rare insight into the many makers they had supported, her answer was not at all surprising. It is a long list indeed, as well as a discussion putting paid to concerns Seidler was only interested in the big names of modern art. The repeated selection from the different echelons of art makers they admired reconfirms the point. Penelope explained how the major international acquisitions came about: "Because of Harry's contacts, ability, and willingness to go abroad, it was not difficult forty years ago to collect important works. ... They were relatively inexpensive and available to acquire."[52] The Morris Louis painting from the *Unfurled* series (1960–61) at the Seidler & Associates office in Milsons Point testifies, as Penelope put it, "to a simpler almost smaller world where such things were possible."[53] Seidler regularly championed lesser-known art makers whose interest in spatial matters he deeply respected.

It is clear now that Seidler's colossal archive—consisting of buildings both grand and modest, architectural drawings, contemporary art, photographs, public, private, and commercial commissions, notes, and private art stock—is a legacy that will continue to have an influence as a national treasure.[54] Belogolovsky recently re-awakened Australian audiences to the quality of the Seidlers' contribution to Australian and international life, and from the subsequent public showing of many unseen paintings, figures, photographs, and models, it was suggested that the Seidlers' true engagement with Australian culture is immense.[55] From that showing, I better understood Belogolovsky's subdued if not concerned tone, just as many others now may appreciate how personal the Seidlers' rigorous engagement with the visual arts had been.

Art Not Nationalism

Shortly after arriving in Australia, Seidler was invited to become a member of the Contemporary Arts Society,[56] given the paintings he collected and the interest in Albers' colour theories among a small but well-informed circle.[57] I would further argue that the Bauhaus tradition was a preference Seidler interpreted in a useful and stylish language that more or less supported abstractionist, not social realist or any nationalistic ideals. It is no less admirable that the Seidlers worked tirelessly over many decades in an environment seeking identity from those using opposing language or dialect much less interested in abstraction let alone non-objective art, art brut, or concrete art.

The local historian Bernard Smith had claimed that imported, ultra-modern influence had been unwanted at the

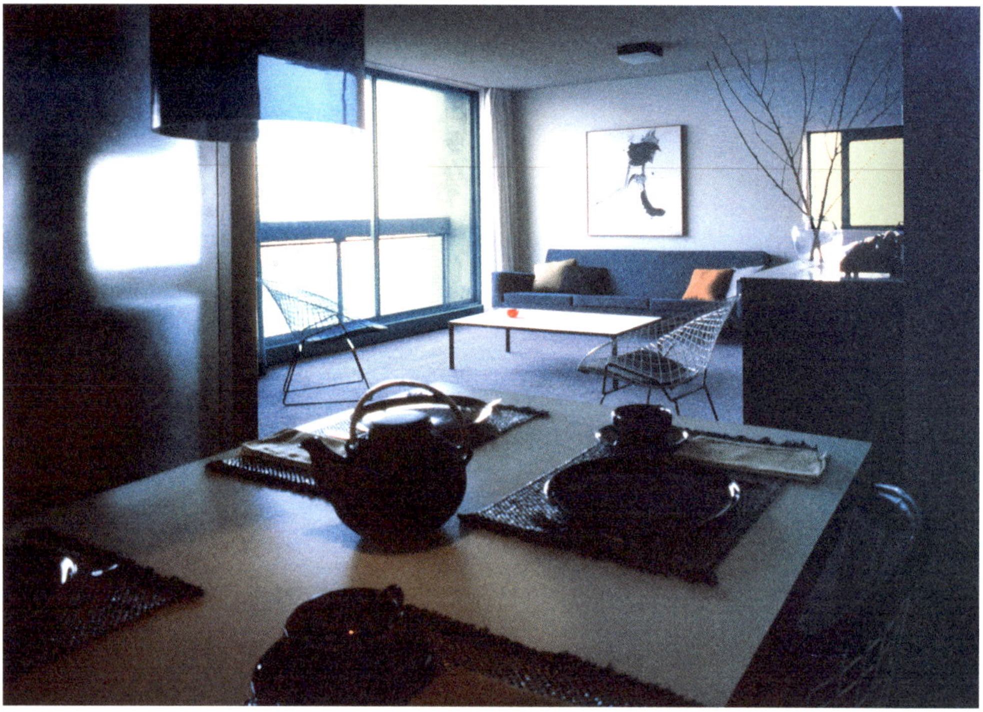

Fig. 14 Peter Upward, *Located*, 1961, Blues Point Tower, Sydney, Photo: Harry Seidler, 1962.

start of Seidler's career, as there were many nationalistically prone voices calling for greater social enrichment, and the subject field of pure abstraction clearly gave no intrinsic value to social realists. Curiously, the term *formalist* has been used liberally to this day by critical voices to define modern artworks that were usually not that.[58] Robertson-Swann, a leading Australian artist, created a major sculptural form that was removed from the Australian Centre for Contemporary Art square for decades. The press and establishment felt it was necessary because it was overtly internationalist.[59] There is no doubt that reflection theory was understood provincially in art circles after Bernard Smith published *Place, Taste, and Tradition*.[60] Regardless, Smith made a point difficult to dismiss concerning homage. In my own words: If an artist is working contemporaneously at the perimeter of major cultural centres or influences, local art styles tend to be caught in reflection. Smith, however, offered a recovery position, claiming that acceptable "exotic" versions occur when local artists act like mystagogues, when they transform myth into cultural truths. Hence an approval of pictorial abstraction is authorized in regional contexts desiring more nationalistic outcomes from a genre.

It is a long way back to what was happening in the late 1960s. In 1968 Clement Greenberg came to Australia and usurped a hard-edged abstractionist artistic circle in a lecture at the University of Sydney organized by Smith. Greenberg announced that of all the regional abstractionist-prone artists he admired, a select few were engaging modernism fittingly, by making modernism's influences exotic.[61] That was the same analysis used approvingly for Smiths' favoured figuratively prone Antipodeans. This matters because leading theorists, among them Smith, published texts in a nationalistic sense renouncing pure abstract art, as well as related influences by proxy, as "un-Australian." Smith was a committed social realist, and his life's work, *Australian Painting,* talks about various ultra-modern artists in a semi-flattering way. His real feelings, however, were expressed in the Antipodean Manifesto, the infamous regional document he co-signed.[62] Importantly, Seidler shared neither sentiment, as his regular selection of Upward and other more expressive abstractionists testifies (Fig. 14).

Signed by an influential circle of abstract, expressionist, and figurative artists and supported by the Sweeney family, the manifesto activists openly condemned the mind-numbing excesses of pure abstraction as a pointless influence on Australian culture.[63] This group of mystagogic poets included Charles Blackman, Arthur Boyd, David Boyd, John Brack, Bob Dickerson, John Perceval, and Clifton Pugh. In opposition, an exhibition was held in 1961 in Sydney by the Sydney Nine group, consisting of Hector Gilliland, Leonard Hessing,

Meadmore, John Olsen, Carl Plate, Stanislaus Rapotec, William Rose, Eric Smith, and Upward, who came together to "assert the seriousness of practitioners of abstraction."[64] Seidler it seems spent his career negotiating a minefield of conflicting opinions while trying to build and then ornament his spectacular buildings. For instance, a modern sculpture by Perry was recommended by Seidler for the Shell House forecourt, completed in 1989. Despite the client, Kevan Gosper, approving it, it is not a public favourite. Conversely, the odd-looking artwork (in the foyer) selected by Shell executives and made by an Antipodean signatory, Boyd, is generally admired. In any event, public distinctions made between abstract art and its antithesis, non-relational pure abstraction, had been made into a conflated truth long before Perry's non-objective art form appeared.

Like many, I first came to Seidler because of the artworks by Le Corbusier, Calder, Albers, Stella and LeWitt featured in his buildings everywhere, but most of all, it is the rich tapestry of period Australian reductive practices I now admire.[65] This posits a straight line from Albers back through Australian art and architecture and must explain why others also find his work, born from a history of known reductive influences, critically inspiring today. Finally, what is being discussed in relation to Seidler's legacy is the arrival of a wave of educated and informed artists working in a lineage, fans who may be best described as a new generation interested in the radical art and architectural languages of the twentieth century.[66] This arrival means that what lays beyond appropriationist theory or latter strategic referentialist models requires discussion.[67] It is therefore more than reasonable to claim that the Seidlers' influence on the Australian contemporary art scene is evident.

1 "In the Mind of the Architect," Australian Broadcasting Corporation, 2000, episode 1, transcript, http://www.abc.net.au/arts/architecture/ep_trn1.htm.

2 In 1918, influenced by cubism's theorizing "intellectual wing" of the Section d'Or or Puteaux group, several artists around Amédée Ozenfant (1886–1966) and Le Corbusier (Charles-Édouard Jeanneret, 1887–1965) found their way to an orderly style with simple and elementary geometric forms close to constructivism. The purists emphasized the typification of the depicted objects in graphic art and painting. Their paintings often show so-called *objets-types* or *objets-standarts* as standardized reproducible basic forms. This illustrates purism's ground-breaking basic assumption that a particular type is inherent to any object. Thus purism and its principle of rationality, instead of ornament, marked the beginning of a new aesthetic that would be carried forth in functionalism.

3 Billy Gruner, "Painting the Object: Recent Formal Australian Painting" (PhD diss., University of Sydney, 2003).

4 Henry-Russell Hitchcock and Philip Johnson, *The International Style: Architecture Since 1922* (New York, 1977).

5 "Frozen Music: Rose Seidler House and the Work of Harry Seidler," documentary directed by Michael Power, 2004, base footage from betacam roll 9, filmed 9 May 2004, The Mint. Transcript and summary transcript, Caroline Simpson Library, The Mint, Sydney Living Museums, pp. 61–62.

6 When Daniel Thomas was appointed to be the first curator of the Art Gallery of NSW in 1959, the Seidler's asked him about suitable artists to place in Seidler's work. He suggested John Coburn, Frank Hodgkinson, and Peter Upward. See Penelope Seidler talk, "Sydney Moderns: Art after House," Art Galley NSW, 31 July 2013, https://www.youtube.com/watch?v=pZVUNdC43js, and email to Polly Seidler, 6 January 2016, passed on to author.

7 It must be noted that Morris Louis's planar transparency and a reorganized view of cubist space was admired in the Seidler office, but not in a public art format as with other artists' work in this list.

8 For an account of Seidler speaking about the black and white maquette versions of *Pillars and Cones*, see *"An Interview with Harry Seidler," Studio Collections Magazine, September–November 1984, p. 28,* as cited *in Vladimir Belogolovsky,* "A Straight Edge and a Circle," 2014, http://sydneylivingmuseums.com.au/stories/straight-edge-and-semicircle. For Seidler discussing the Stella works at Grosvenor Place, see Royal Australian Institute of Architects, NSW Chapter, "Harry Seidler: Sulman Award, 1991, Grosvenor Place," film, at 10:32–11:33 minutes, https://youtu.be/Q1tvvy9ZdwE.

9 See *Max Dupain: Australian Photographs* (1987). The Dupain images are courtesy of Eric Seirins, custodian of Dupain's digitized images of Seidler's work. The State Library of New South Wales is official custodian of all Dupain's architectural photographs. Many thanks to Polly Seidler, who kindly located images, sought out artwork titles, processed copyright permissions, and digitized requests.

10 "Paying the Freight for the Paris Opening," *Sydney Morning Herald,* 30 July 1977, p. 13. One official letter mentions a donation of a work, *Kinga, The Legendary Crocodile,* by the Arnhem Land artist Curley Barrdjungka, but there is no photo. The document, from the Aboriginal Affairs department, approves the transport of a number of aboriginal art works, but they are not named. The document cites, for instance, "5 bark paintings" and so on. Another letter, from G. H. Setchell, mentions several paintings and objects sent to the embassy, including *Tinari Cycle,* by Djangala; *Totemic Spirit,* by Jambanah; *Ceremonial Figure,* by Apuatini. Librarian Services at the State Library of New South Wales (NSW) provided this information from the Seidler embassy art files, MLMSS 7078/14-15.

11 Harry Seidler project files, 1959–81, 1976–79, "Paris Art," MLMSS 7078/14, correspondence and papers concerning artworks for the Australian embassy, Paris, Harry Seidler Collection, Mitchell Library, State Library NSW.

12 Harry Seidler project files, 1951–81, "Paris Art," MLMSS 7078/14-15. Thanks to Polly Seidler and Librarian Services, State Library NSW, for locating this.

13 The regionalism debate in Australian art is suitably covered in this text. Geoffrey Joseph Wallis and Ron Robertson-Swann, *Peril in the Square: The Sculpture That Challenged a City* (Briar Hill, 2004).

14 Harry Seidler, *Internment: The Diaries of Harry Seidler, May 1940–October 1941,* ed. Janis Wilton (Sydney, 1986); also see Helen O'Neil, *A Singular Vision: Harry Seidler* (Sydney, 2013).

15 Harry Seidler, "Our Heritage of Modern Building," in *Houses, Interiors and Projects* (Sydney, 1954), p. ix. For a summary of what Seidler learned at Harvard, see the lecture that he gave at the University of New South Wales, 26 June 1980, https://youtu.be/8-UbE2nnvJo.

16 Patrick Troy, *Accommodating Australians: Commonwealth Government Involvement in Housing* (Sydney, 2012).

17 Nicholas Fox Webber and Martin Filler, *Josef + Anni Albers: Designs for Living* (London, 2004); Martin Duberman, *Black Mountain College: An Exploration in Community* (Evanston, Ill., 2009).

18 Josef Albers, *Interaction of Color* (New Haven, 2007).

19 Peter McMahon and Christine Cipriani, *Cape Cod Modern: Midcentury Architecture and Community on the Outer Cape* (New York, 2014).

20 Harry Seidler, "Painting toward Architecture," Architecture" (RAIA journal, forerunner to *Architecture Australia*) 37, no. 10 (1949): 120–22.

21 John Nixon, ed., *Young Blood: Notes on Art Practice* (Melbourne, 1983).

22 Ibid., p. 4. Also see SNO Contemporary Art Projects, www.sno.org.au.

23 Australian Centre for Concrete Art, www.ac4ca.net.

24 *Richard Leplastrier: Spirit of Nature Wood Architecture Award, 2004,* ed. Kristiina Lehtimaki and Petri Neuvonen, trans. Griffith Gareth (Helsinki, 1999).

25 Seidler, "Painting toward Architecture."

26 Author interview with Penelope Seidler, Milsons Point, NSW, Australia, March 2015.

27 "Harry Seidler: A Life," Australian Broadcasting Corporation, documentary, 1994.

28 Vladimir Belogolovsky, *Harry Seidler: Lifework* (Rizzoli, New York, 2014).

29 Edward W. Said, *Orientalism* (New York, 1979).

30 This was at a time when the National Gallery of Australia in Canberra was under construction. Seidler worked out the terms of the loaned artwork with the director, James Mollison.

31 Paul Taylor, *Anything Goes: Art in Australia, 1970–80* (Melbourne, 1984). Taylor curated the landmark 1982 exhibition *Popism* at the National Gallery of Victoria.

32 Kirstie Beaven and Rebecca Ward, "Tate Debate: When Is Appropriation Homage and When Is It Plagiarism?," 18 October 2012, http://www.tate.org.uk/context-comment/blogs/tate-debate-when-appropriation-homage-and-when-it-plagiarism.

33 As evident in the exhibition *Harry Seidler: Painting toward Architecture,* Museum of Sydney, 1 November 2014–8 March 2015, curated by Vladimir Belogolovsky and Caroline Butler-Bowden; John Nixon in conversation with the author at the Rose Seidler House, 2004.

34 The Robert Owen MLC Centre artwork brief was dated March 2006, just after Seidler died. At Penelope Seidler's suggestion, proposals were sought from Owen, Sydney Ball, and Lin Utzon.

35 Author interview with Robert Owen, Sydney/Melbourne, March 2015. The transcript is the author's interpretation of the noisy, taped interview. Robert Owen dedicated his artwork *Interlude–Double Wave* to Harry Seidler AC.

36 Ibid.

37 Peter Brooker, ed., *Modernism/Postmodernism* (London, 1992).

38 Center for Contemporary Non-Objective Art, http://www.ccnoa.org/Catalogue-presentation.

39 PS, www.psprojectspace.nl.

40 Minus Space, www.minusspace.com.

41 Non-Objectif Sud, www.nonobjectifsud.org.

42 Refer to the UND (meaning "next") extended series of cross-curatorial exhibitions in Europe between 2004 and 2009. Tilman Hoeful, Jan Van der Ploeg, and the author invited artists from all over the world to participate in events held in various cities. The artist-run events were like a convention, where artists could meet and get to know each other. Search the project space archives of CCNOA (Brussels), PS (Amsterdam), SNO (Sydney), and NOS (southern France), for the scant details recorded.

43 Author interview with Owen, Sydney/Melbourne, March 2015. The transcript is the author's interpretation of the noisy taped interview.

44 Ibid.

45 *Concrete Art in Europe after 1945: The Peter C. Ruppert Collection,* ed. Museum im Kulturspeicher et al. (Bonn, 2007); Stephen Bann, *The Tradition of Constructivism* (New York, 1990).

46 Gruner, "Painting the Object."

47 Charles Jenks, *Post-modernism: The New Classicism in Art and Architecture* (New York, 1990).

48 Tom Mallory, "Top 10 Buildings: Women in Architecture," *Huffington Post,* 6 June 2011, http://www.huffingtonpost.com/tom-mallory/top-10-buildings-women-de_b_844239.html.

49 Pier Luigi Nervi, *Esthetics and Technology in Building* (Cambridge, Mass., 1965).

50 Meadmore was the first artist suggested for the sculpture for Australia Square in the early 1960s, but the client did not approve. Later Calder was selected.
Alice Spigelman, *Almost Full Circle: Harry Seidler: A Biography* (Sydney, 2001), p. 274. Aspden, Ball, and Christmann were selected for the Paris embassy in the 1970s. Aspden is also in the Shell House, and there is a Ball *Stain* painting in the Capita building on the executive floor, both from 1989. Johnson is in the Waverly Civic Centre (now City of Monash), from 1985. Works by Firth-Smith, Martin, and Watson were selected for the executive floor of the Shell House. Penelope Seidler was on that project's art selection commitee. Seidler commissioned the John Olsen tapestry *Yellow Summer,* 1966, by John Olsen for Australia Sqare, refer to http://www.deutscherandhackett.com/auction/12-fine-art-auction/lot/yellow-summer-1966. There is also a 1956 John Olsen artwork called *Composition,* part of *Direction 1* paintings, in Seidler's Jack Meller House, Double Bay NSW finished 1958.
Harry Seidler is on record as saying he liked the work of Fred Williams. Refer to "Postcard from Harry Seidler, Architect", *Look* (magazine of Art Gallery Society), special "Australian Art" issue, (April 2000), p. 33. Although the Seidlers met Williams, his living in Melbourne prevented his work from being readily available for Seidler's designs. There were also other Australian artists whose works Seidler incorporated in his work.

51 Author interview with Penelope Seidler, Milsons Point, NSW, Australia, March 2015.

52 Ibid.

53 Ibid.

54 The main Seidler archive is the Harry Seidler Collection, Mitchell Library, State Library NSW. Other smaller collections are at Seidler & Associates, Milsons Point, NSW, and Max Dupain & Associates Archive, 9689-6, State Library, NSW. Penelope Seidler also has some personal letters from 1970 onwards and personal sketches from the early 1980s at her home.

55 Vladimir Belogolovsky, *Harry Seidler: Lifework* (New York 2014).

56 Interview with Harry and Penelope Seidler, 12 May 2001, Rose Seidler House, with Colleen Morris, Andrew Mitchell, and Linda Rector, transcript, 12 May 2001, p. 88, Caroline Simpson Library and Research Collection, The Mint, Sydney Living Museums.

57 Albers, *Interaction of Color.*

58 Rhianna Daniels, "Boccaccio and the Italian Novella," college coursework, University of Bristol, 2012.

59 Shane Green, "Should It Be Back to Square One?," *Age,* 17 August 2013.

60 Bernard Smith, *Place, Taste, and Tradition: A Study of Australian Art since 1788* (New York, 1979).

61 Clement Greenberg, "Avant-Garde Attitudes: New Art in Sixties" (Power Institute of Fine Arts Lecture, University

of Sydney, 1969). Of note, the Seidlers entertained Clement Greenberg at Killara, at the request of Smith.

62 Bernard Smith, *Australian Painting, 1788–1960* (Melbourne, 1962); Bernard Smith, *The Antipodean Manifesto: Essays in Art and History* (Melbourne, 1976), p. 165.

63 The Sweeney family were patrons of the arts. The slogan for the Heide Museum remains "Heide—Making History." Heide features works of the most famous Australian Antipodeans and other abstractionist works. See www.heide.com.au/assets/files/Education/HeideEdResourceMakingHistory12.pdf.

64 Deborah Clark, "Antipodeans: Challenge and Response in Australian Art, 1955–65," National Gallery of Australia, http://nga.gov.au/exhibitions/antipodeans/index.htm.

65 I ran SNO from 2003 to 2013 and took many international visitors around Sydney to see Seidler buildings and the artworks on the grounds and in foyers commissioned by him. The interest came through a visual arts connection as we discussed the significance of his works or the relational legacy of works he introduced. For instance, Jan Van Der Pleog, from PS projects in Amsterdam, and I did the walk many times, long before it was as popular as it is today. At that time, it was a small circle of visual artists looking at the connections to purist histories, art concrete, and the like who read the work and buildings as meaningful to a new wave of enthusiasts.

66 Billy Gruner, Sydney presentation of the exhibition *What Is Post-Formalism?*, originally at ParisCONCRET in 2009, SNO Archives www.sno.org.au; and Minus Space, Brooklyn. PS Amsterdam, CCNOA Brussels, NOS France, ParisCONCRET, and other related non-objective art spaces archives provide an array of new material on contemporary non-objective art and artists lists.

67 Yves-Alain Bois, *Painting as Model* (Cambridge, Mass., 1993.) Here various strategies are outlined concerning how the language of art changes via its use in other intents.

III

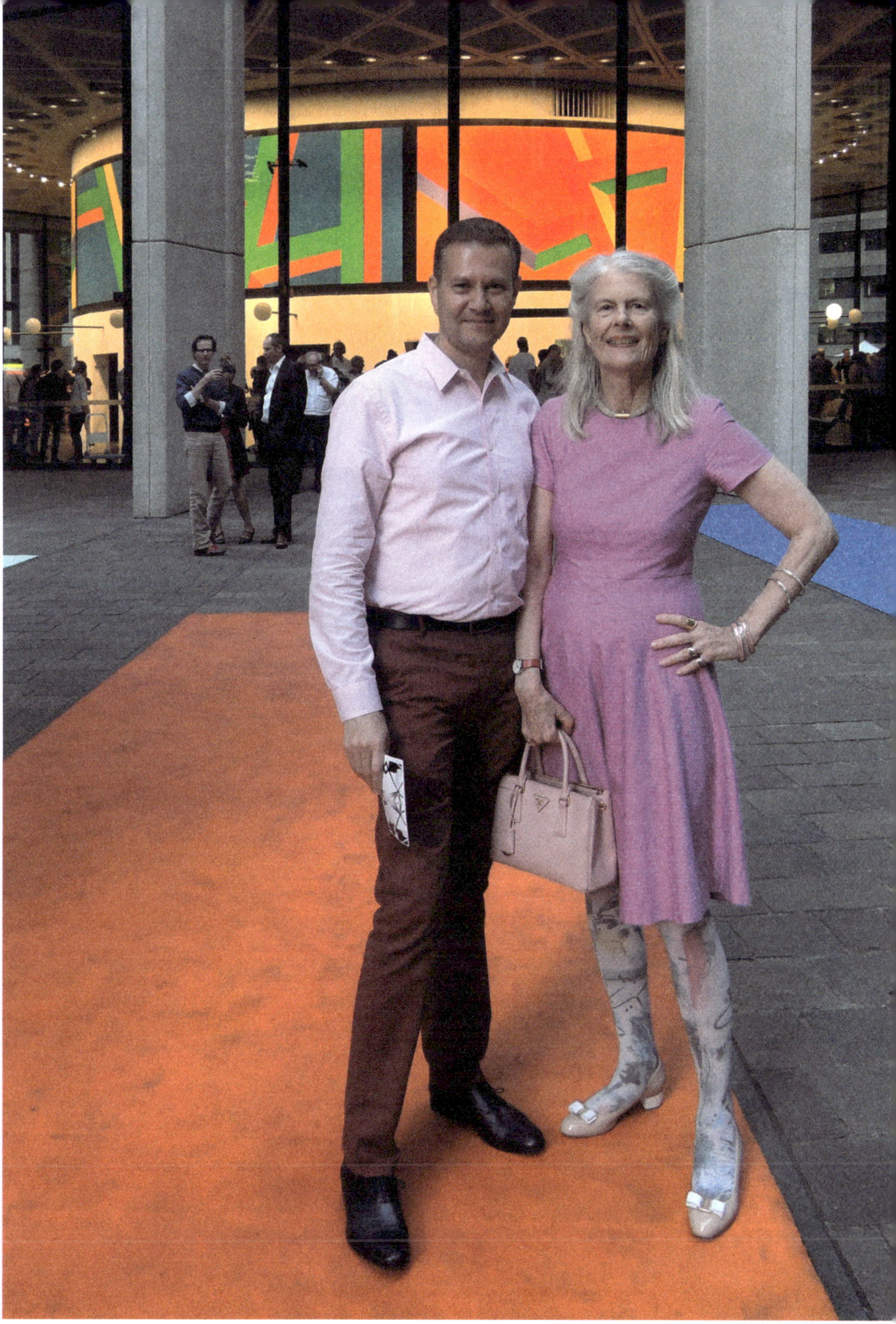

Penelope Seidler and Vladimir Belogolovsky standing on *Floor Painting*, by Nina and Elena Tory-Henderson, Australia Square (in the backrground *Bars of Colour*, 2002, by Sol LeWitt), Photo: Alex Wisser, 2014.

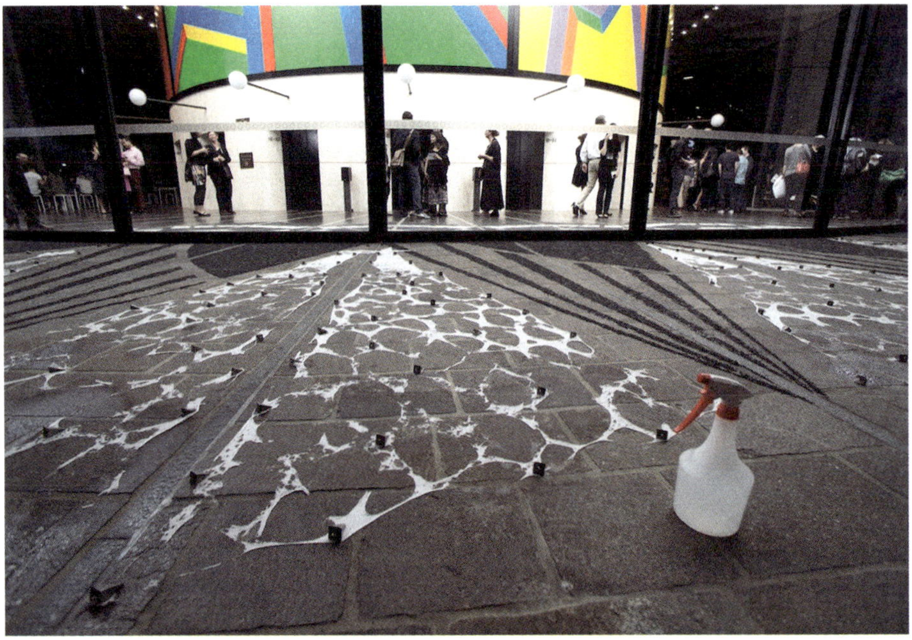

Ainslie Murray, *The Matter of Voids*, Australia Square (in the backrground *Bars of Colour*, 2002, by Sol LeWitt), Photo: Ian Hobbs, 2014.

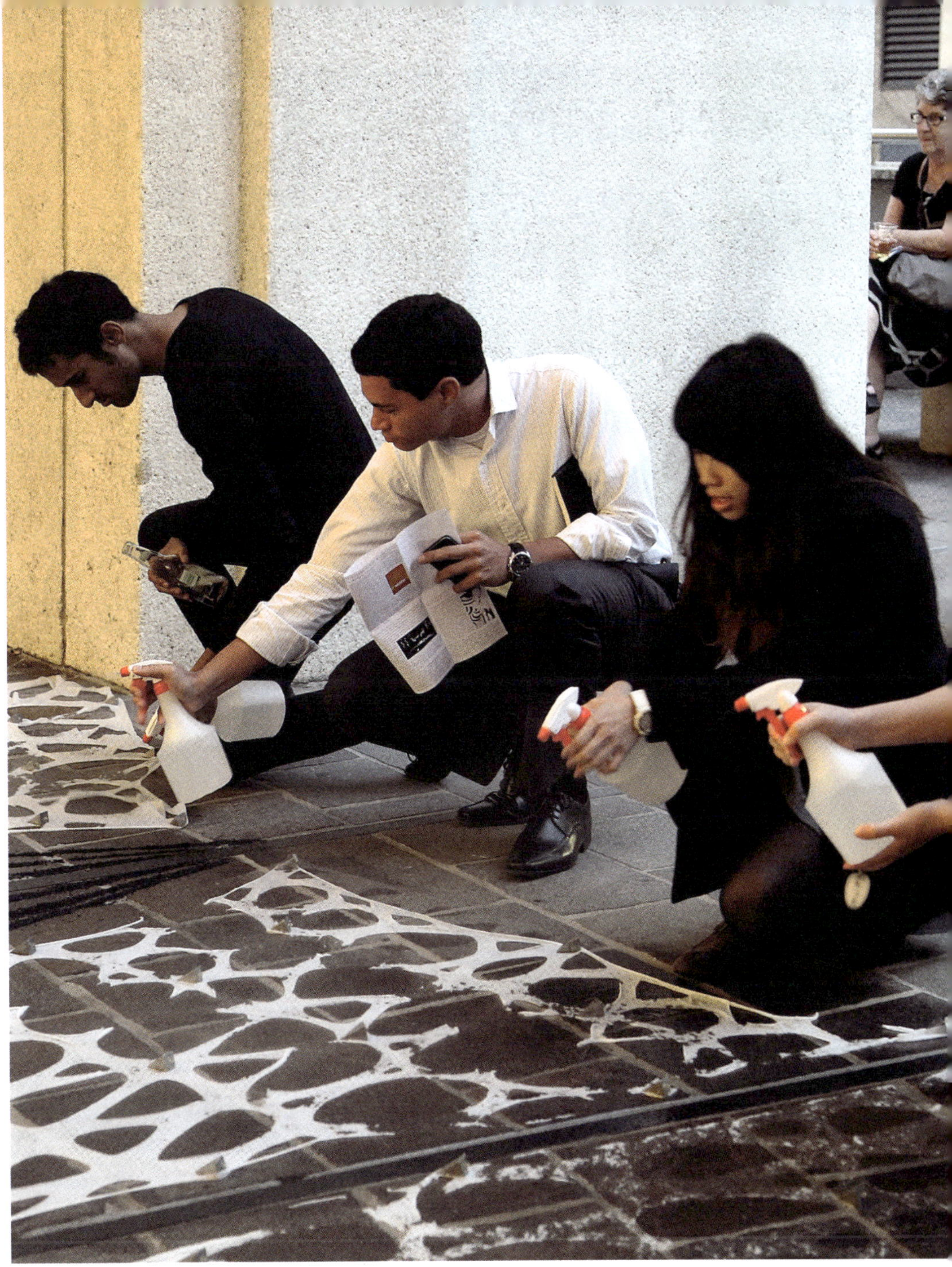

Ainslie Murray, *The Matter of Voids*, Australia Square,
Photo: Vinchy Yi Wu, 2014.

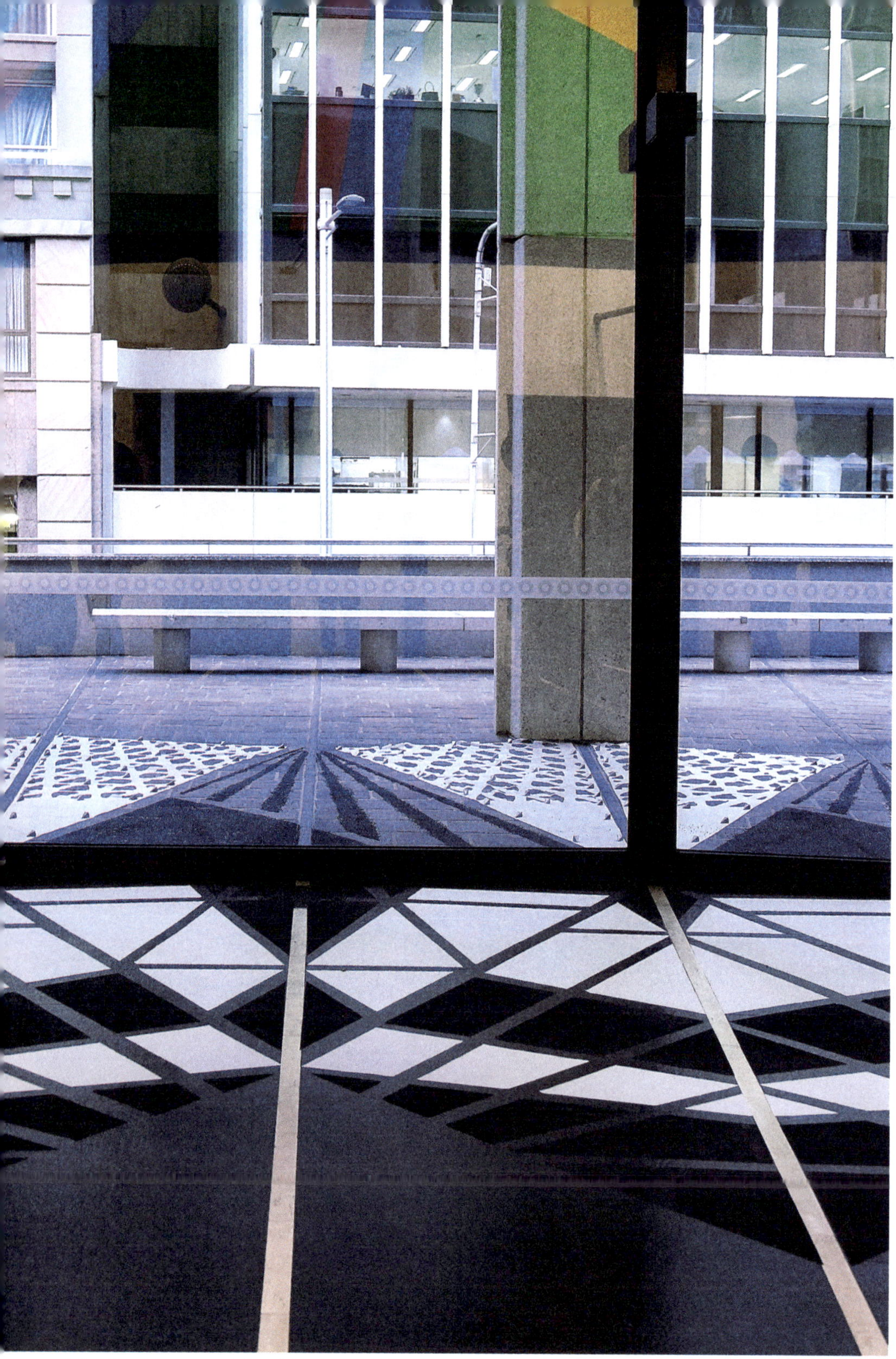

Ainslie Murray, *The Matter of Voids*, Australia Square,
Photo: Alex Wisser, 2014.

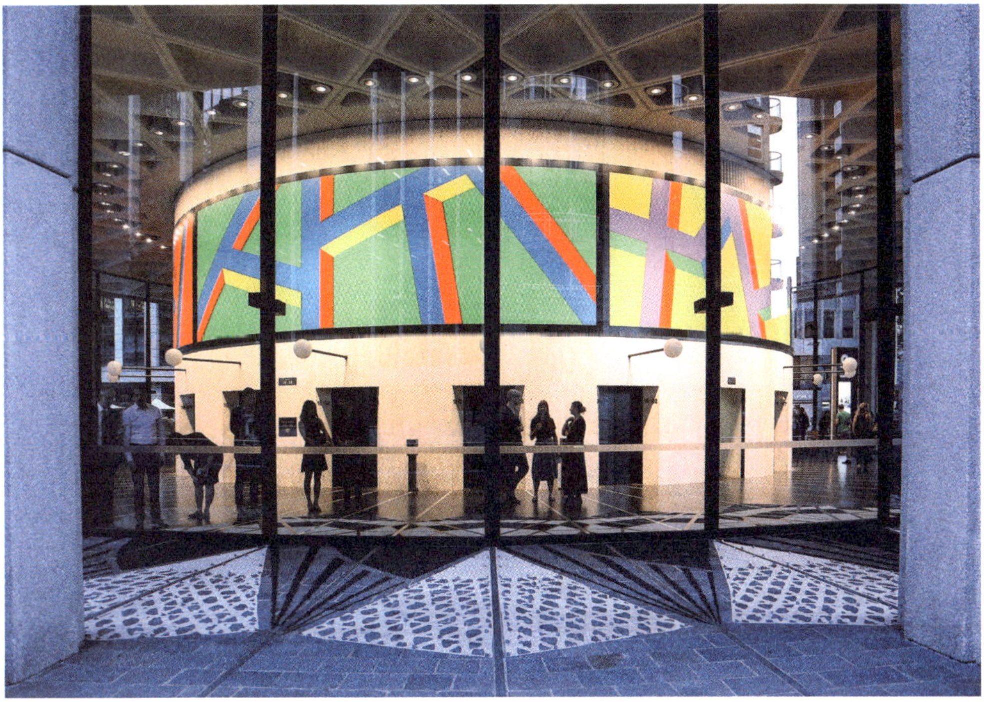

Ainslie Murray, *The Matter of Voids*, Australia Square
(in the backrground *Bars of Colour*, 2002, by Sol LeWitt),
Photo: Vinchy Yi Wu, 2014.

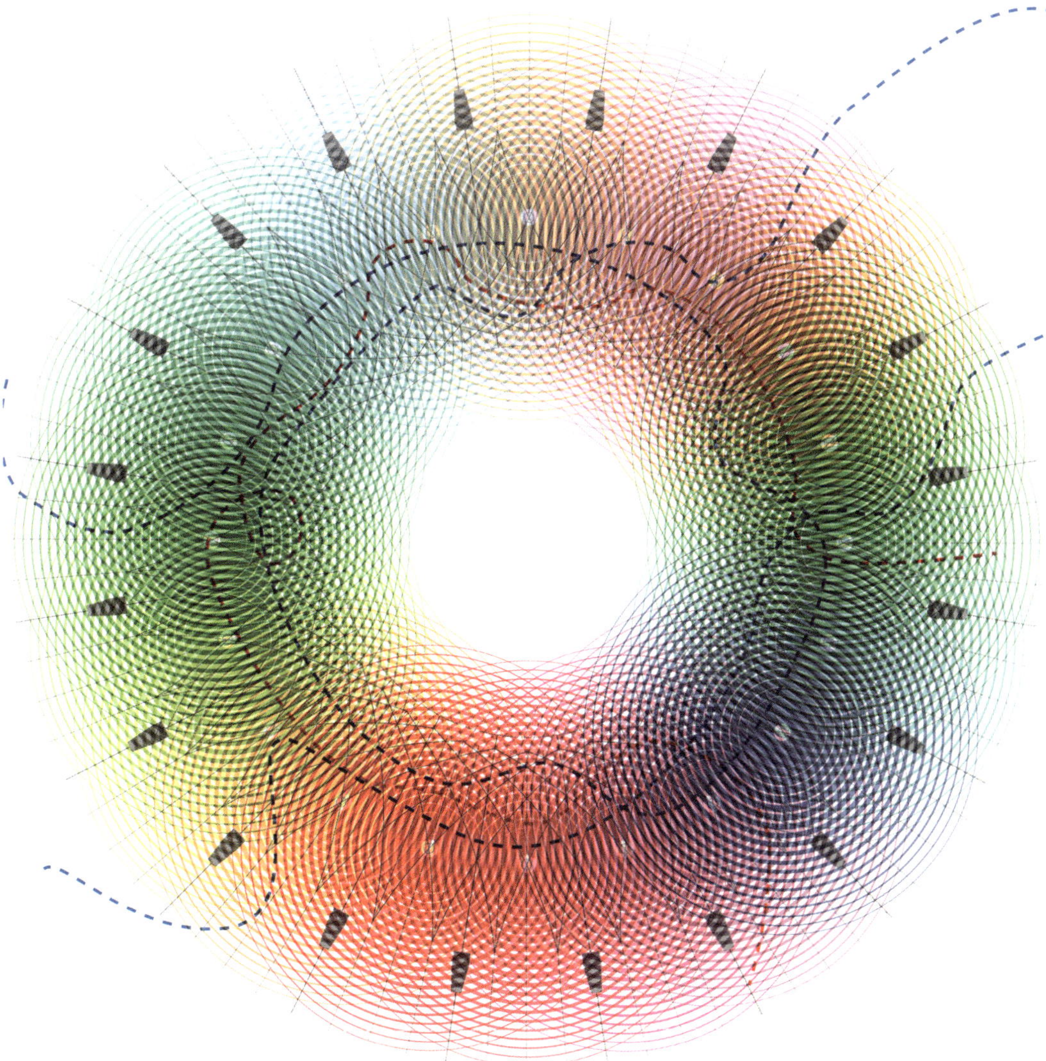

Lindsay Webb and Amanda Cole, *You Are Hear*, Australia Square, 2014. Diagram showing the distribution of loudspeakers as sound sources creating an evolving experiential harmonic map of the lobby in which the flâneuring audience can "play the gradient."

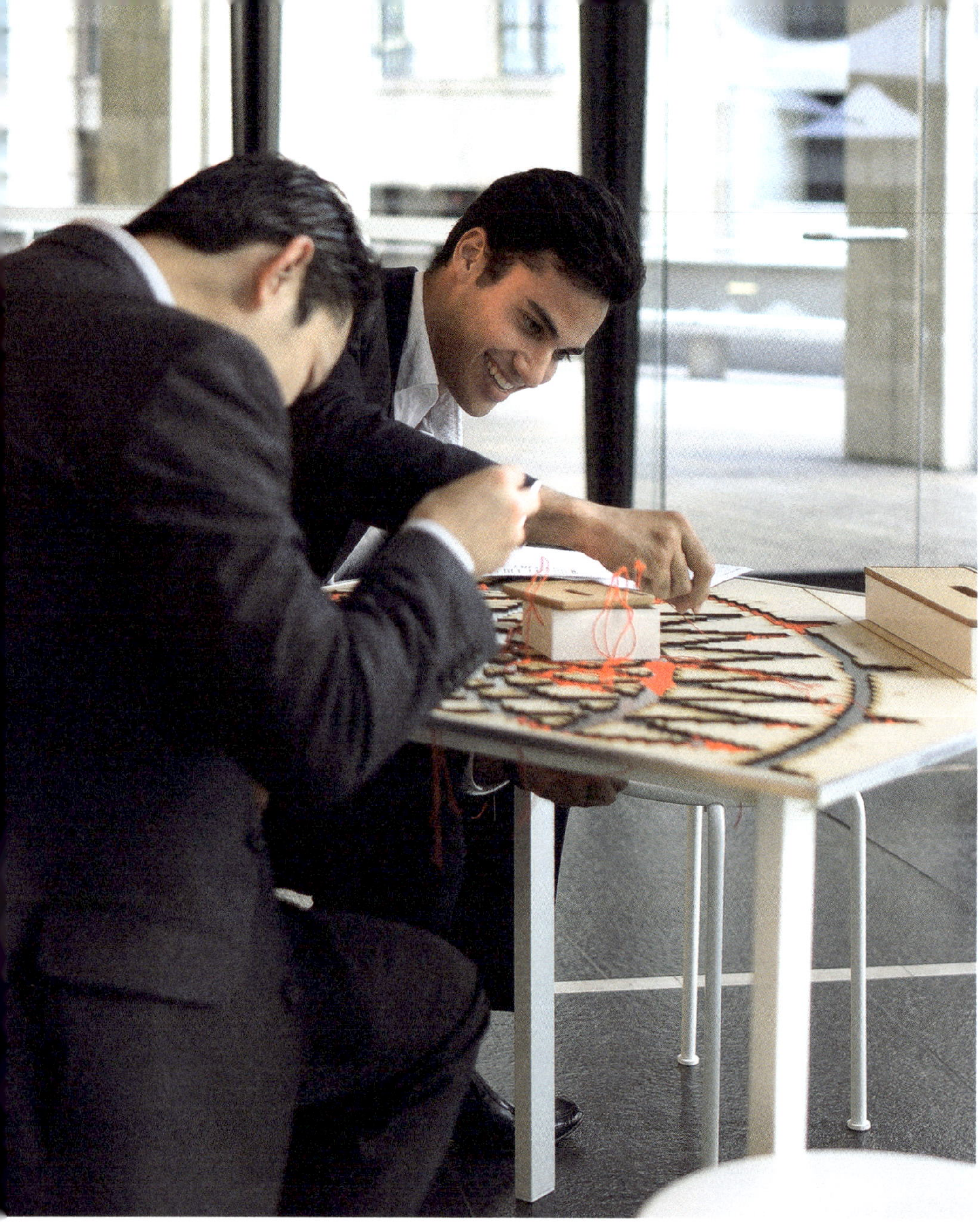

Cottage Industries, *Haus der Frau*, Australia Square,
Photo: Jung Ming, 2014.

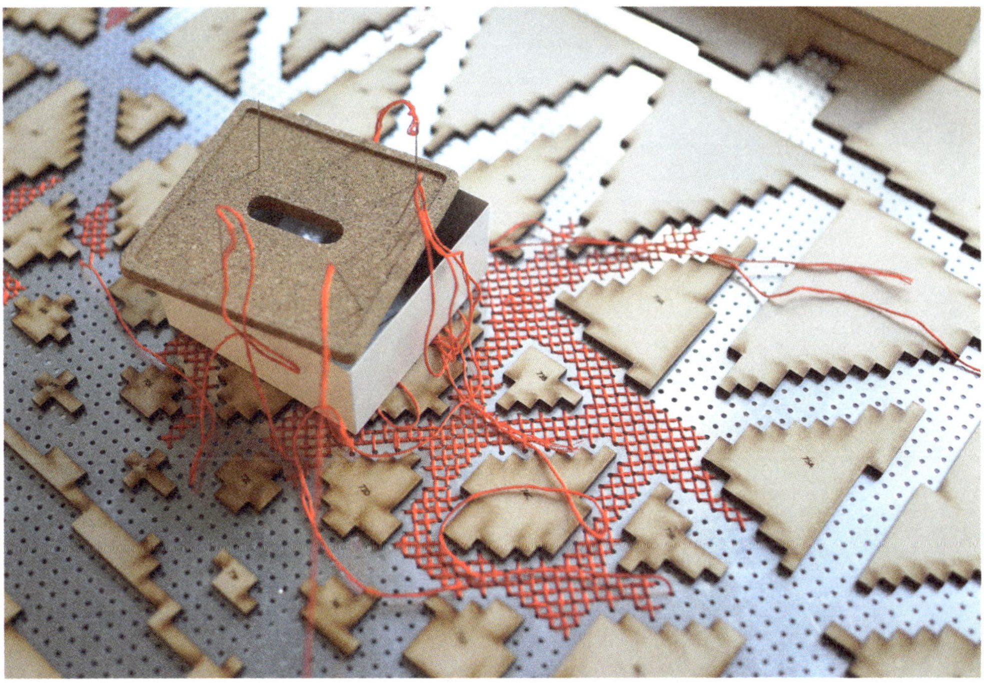

Cottage Industries, *Haus der Frau*, Australia Square,
Photo: Jung Ming, 2014.

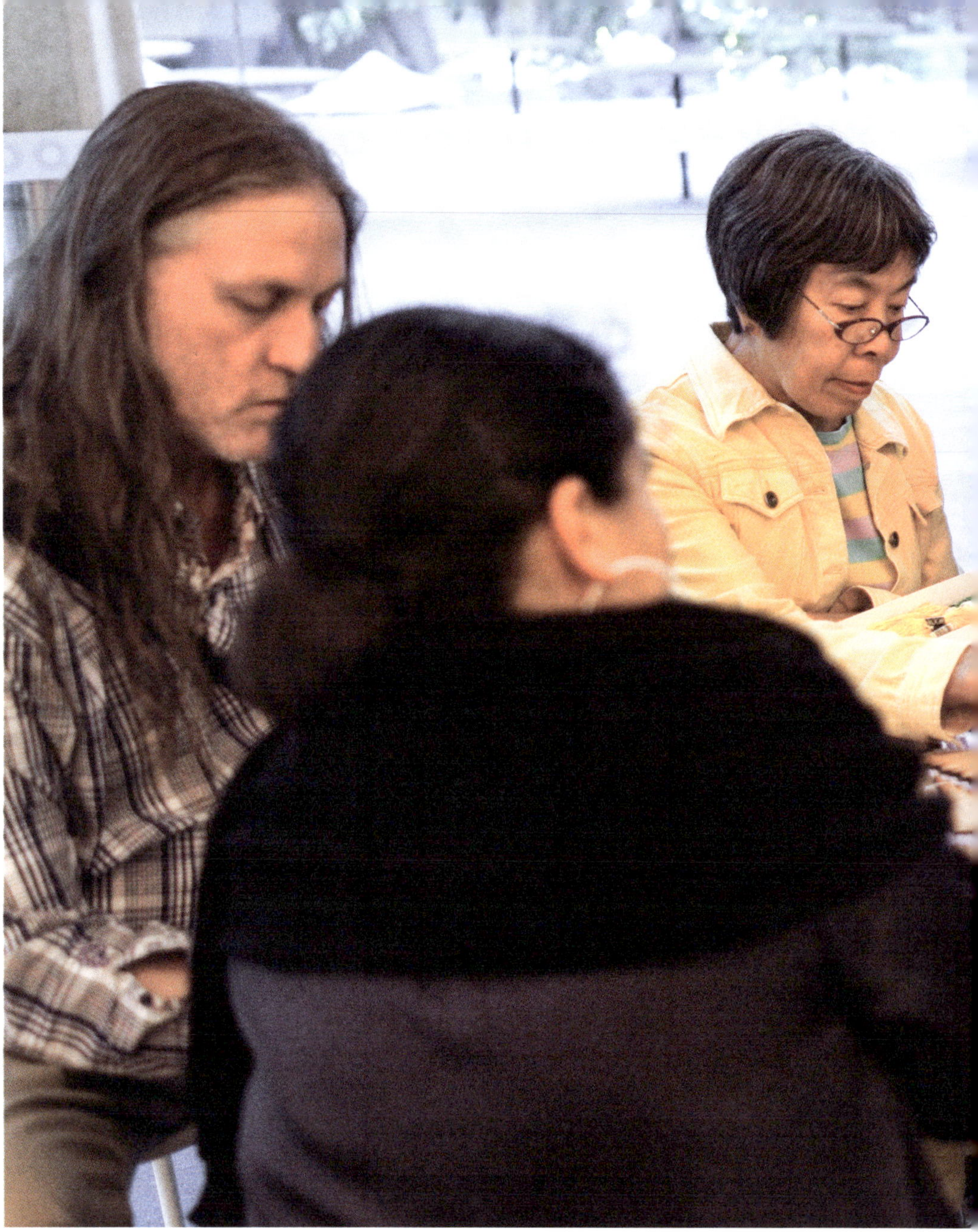

Cottage Industries, *Haus der Frau*, Australia Square,
Photo: Jung Ming, 2014.

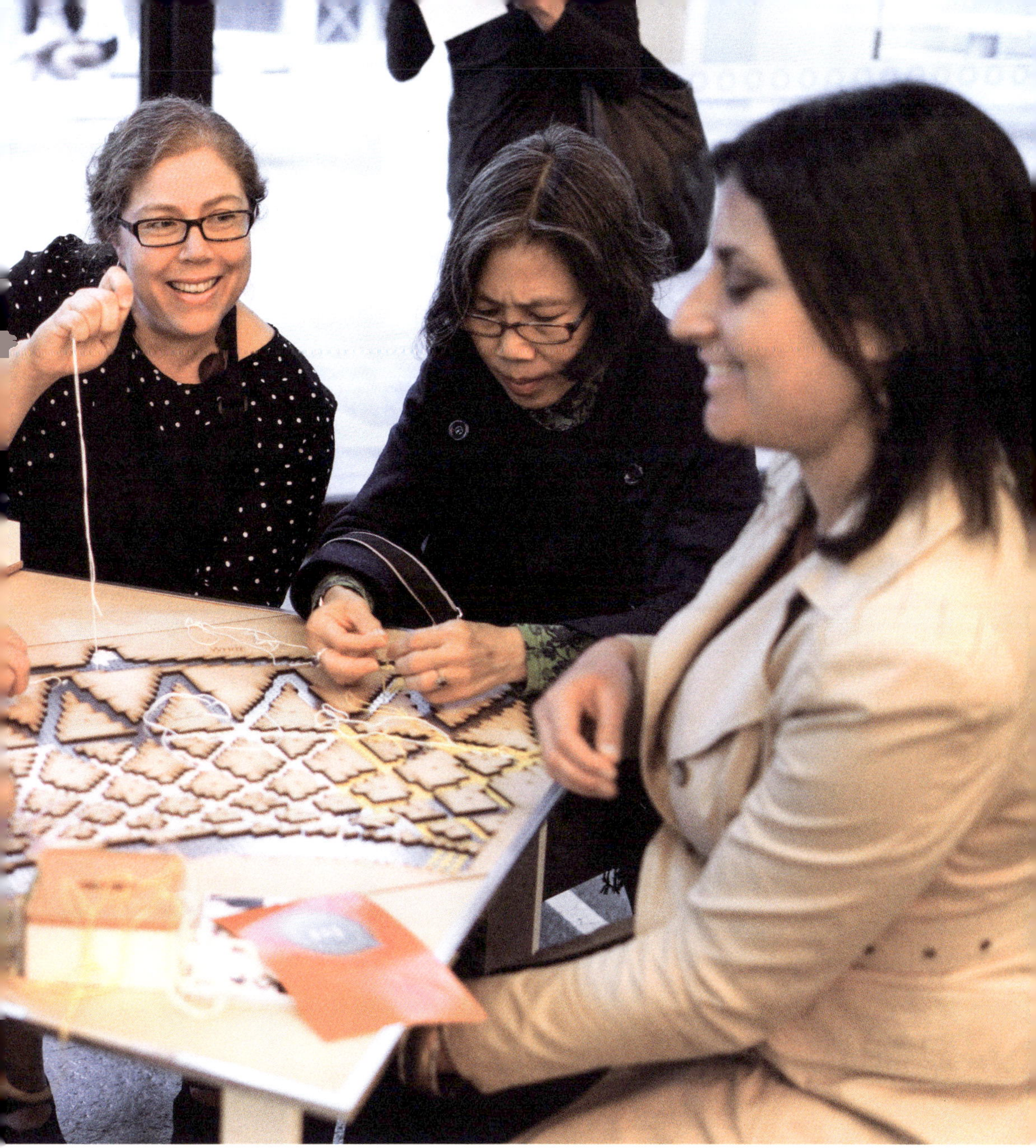

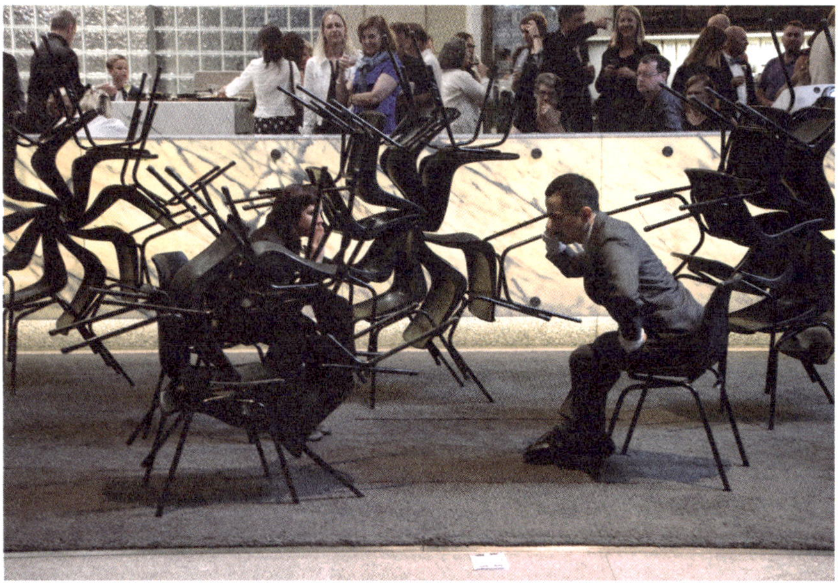

Ryuichi Fujimura and Kate Sherman performing in the installation *Take a Seat,* by Bellemo & Cat, Capita Centre, 9 Castlereagh Street, Photo: Vinchy Yi Wu, 2014.

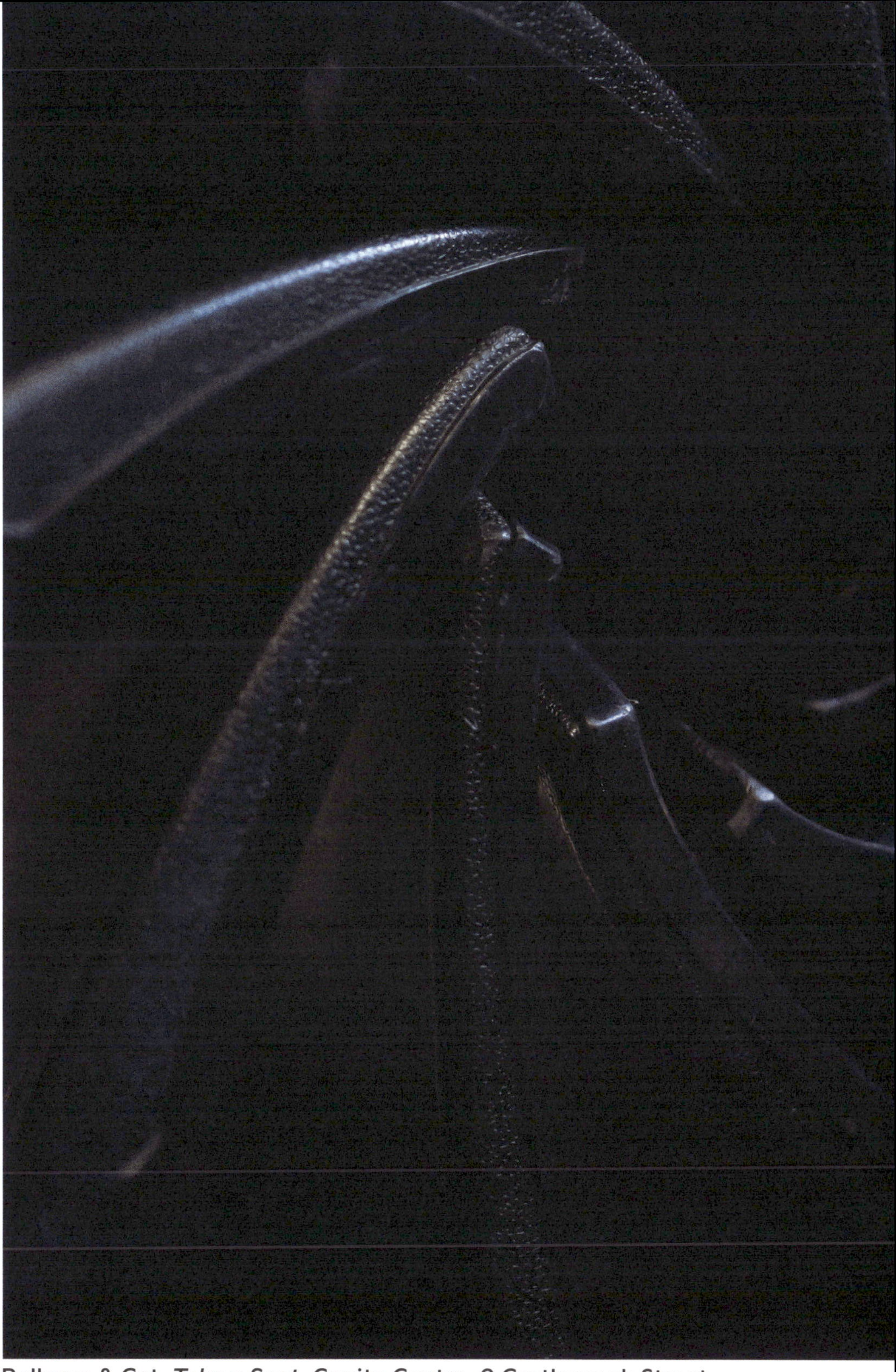

Bellemo & Cat, *Take a Seat,* Capita Centre, 9 Castlereagh Street, Photo: Jung Ming, 2014.

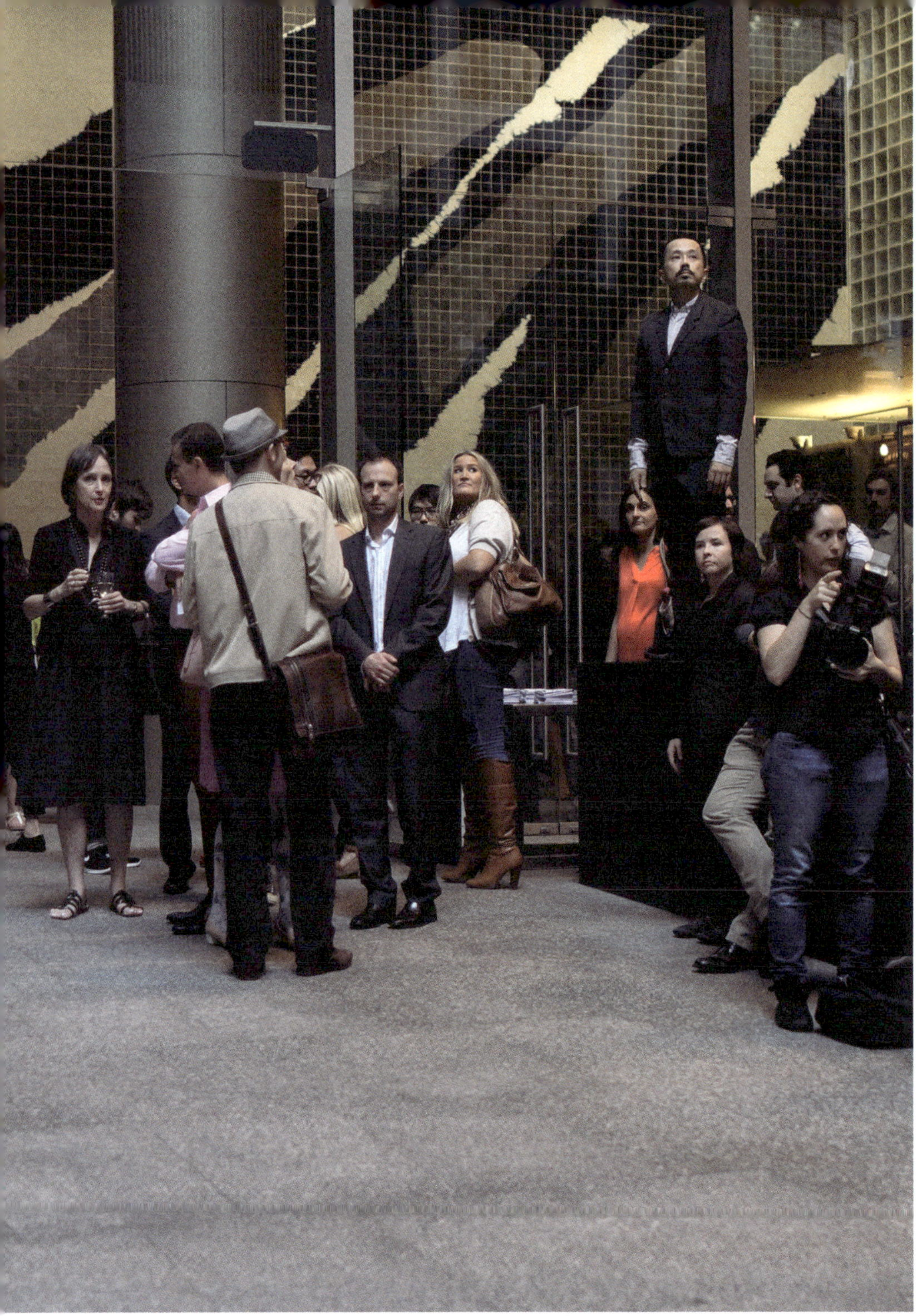

Ryuichi Fujimura and Kate Sherman performing *Under Harry's Circumstances,* Capita Centre, 9 Castlereagh Street (in the background mural by Lin Utzon), Photo: Jung Ming, 2014.

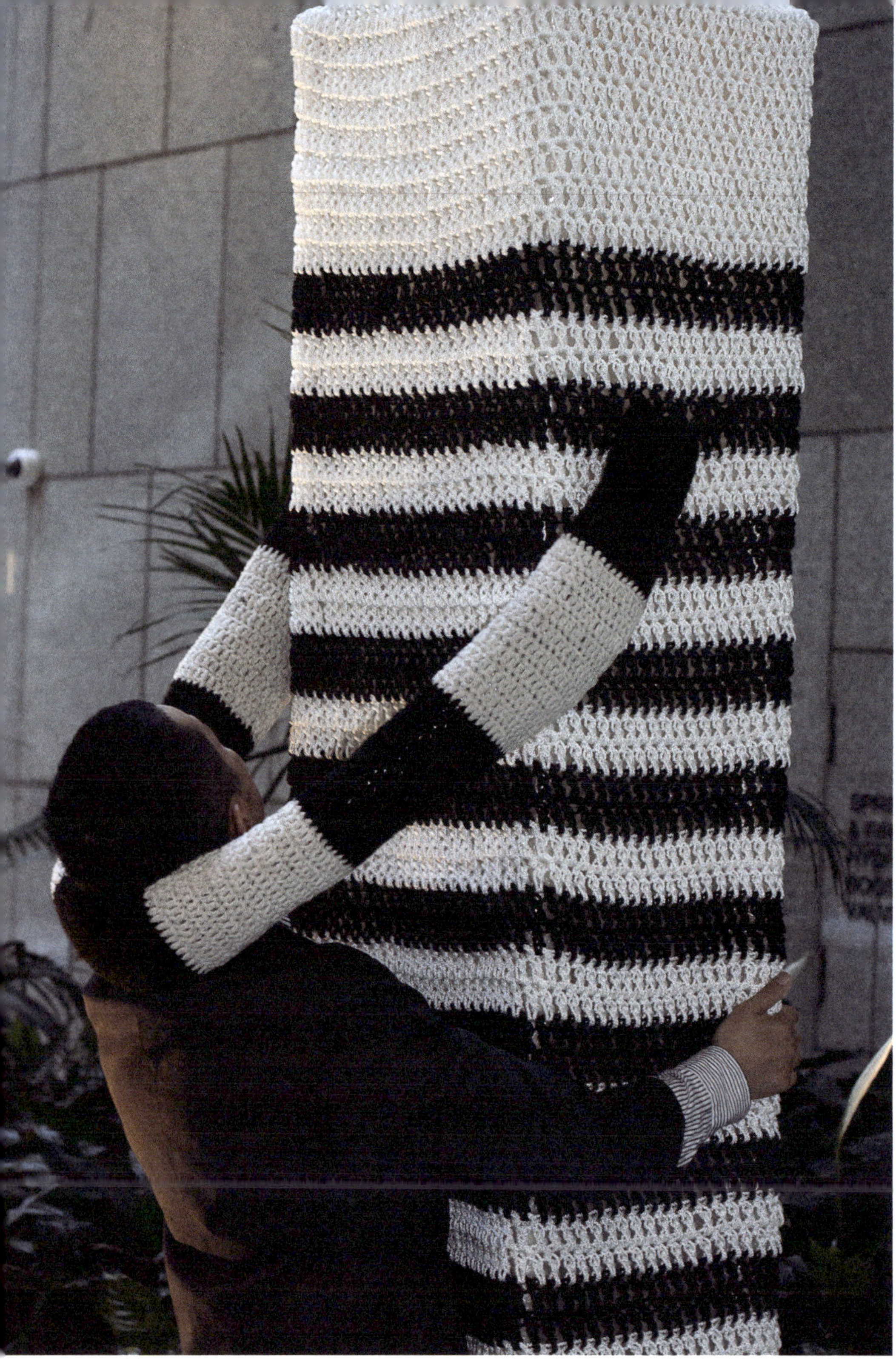

Tina Fox, *Sentries* (with Ryuichi Fujimura), Capita Centre, 9 Castlereagh Street, Photo: Olivia Govan, 2014.

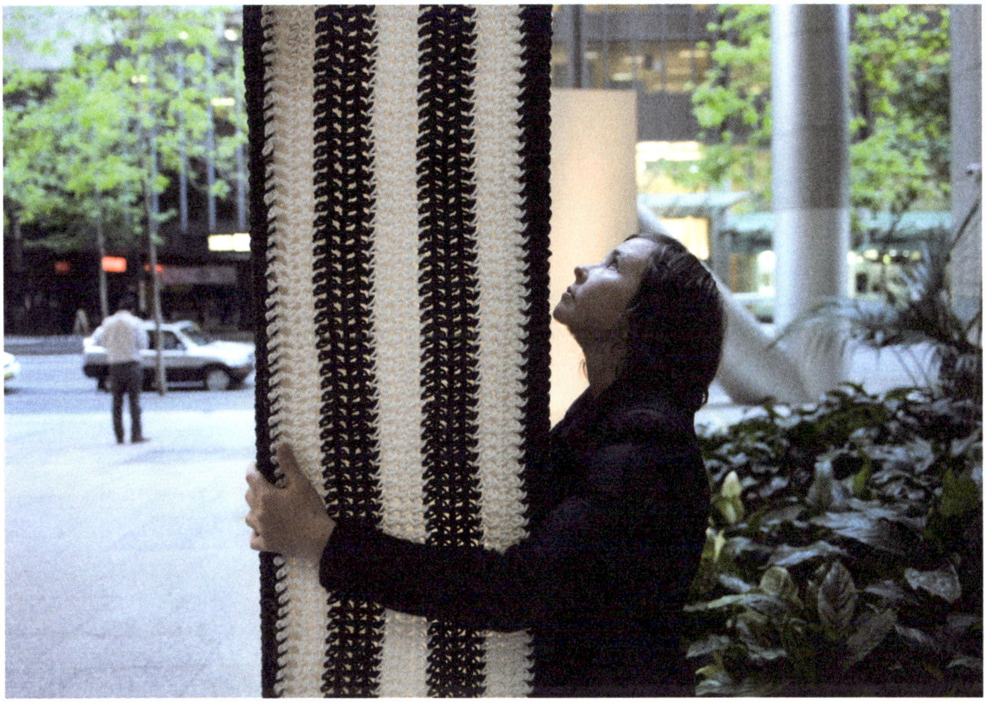

Tina Fox, *Sentries* (with Kate Sherman), Capita Centre, 9 Castlereagh Street, Photo: Alex Wisser, 2014.

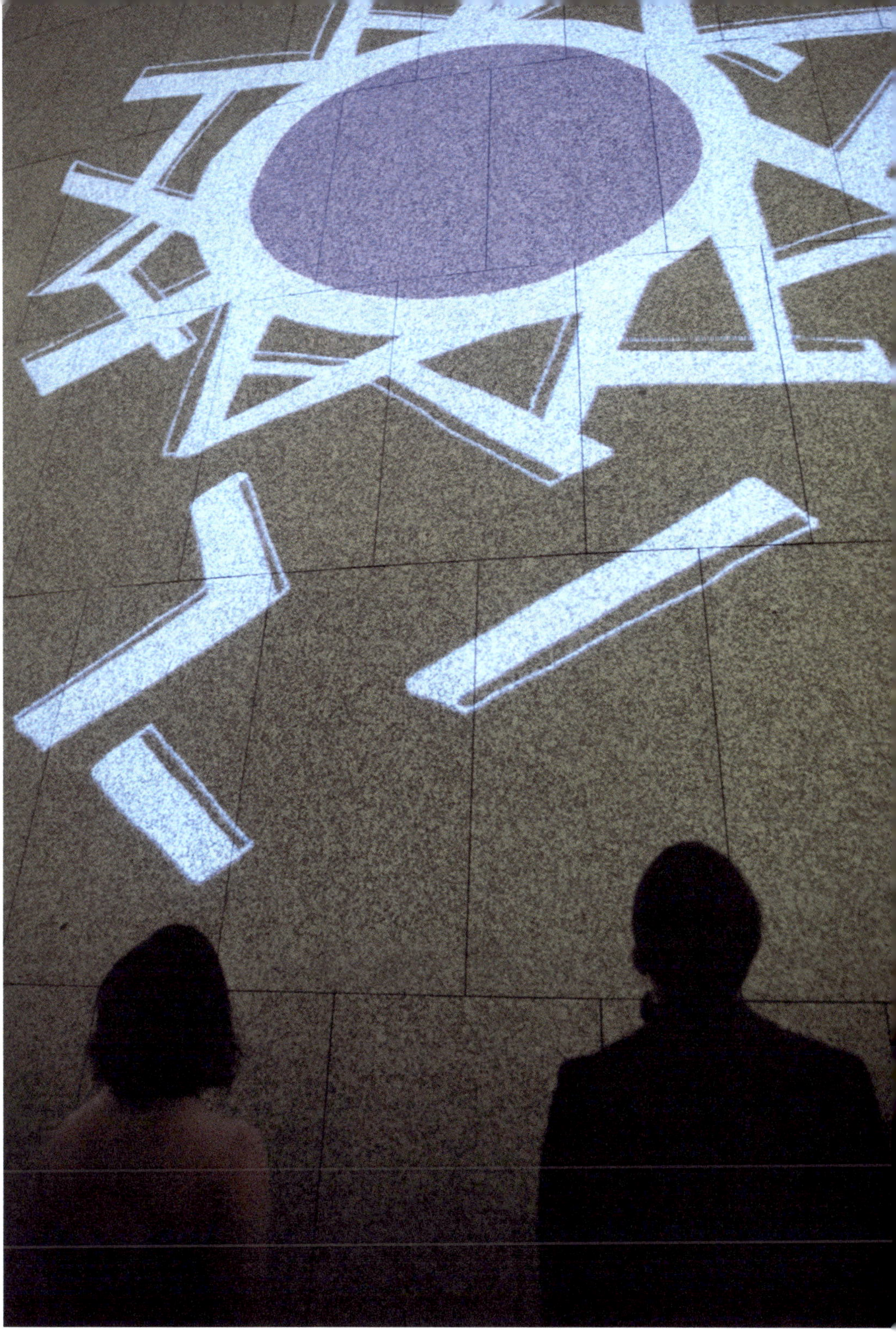

Ryuichi Fujimura and Kate Sherman standing before *Collaborative Mapping,* by Kate Dunn and Phillip Gough, Grosvenor Place, Photo: Alex Wisser, 2014.

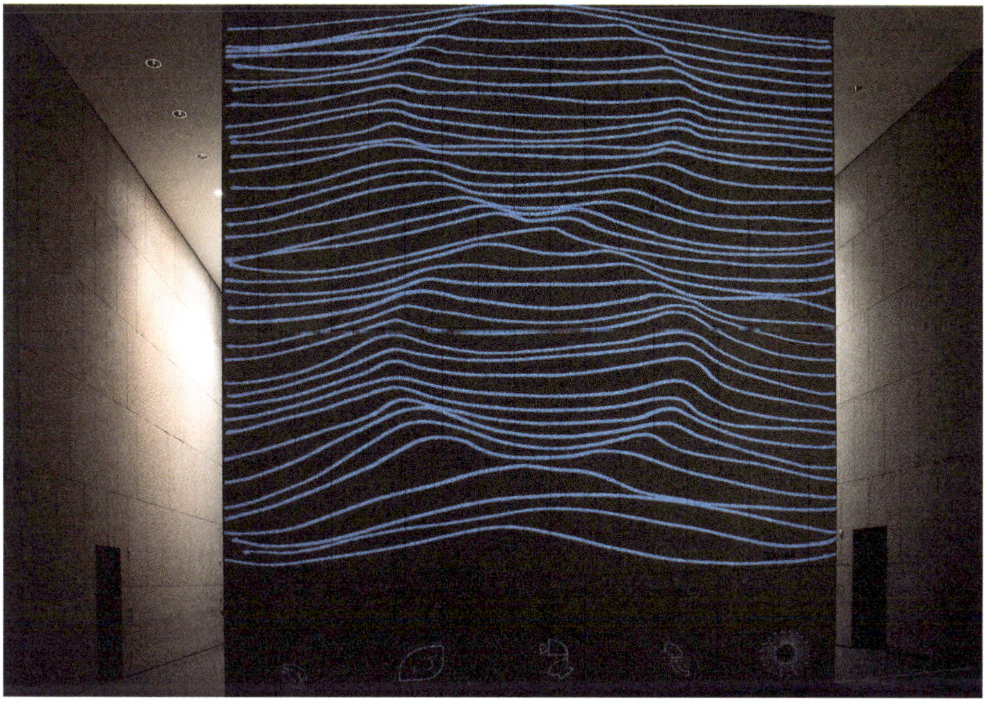

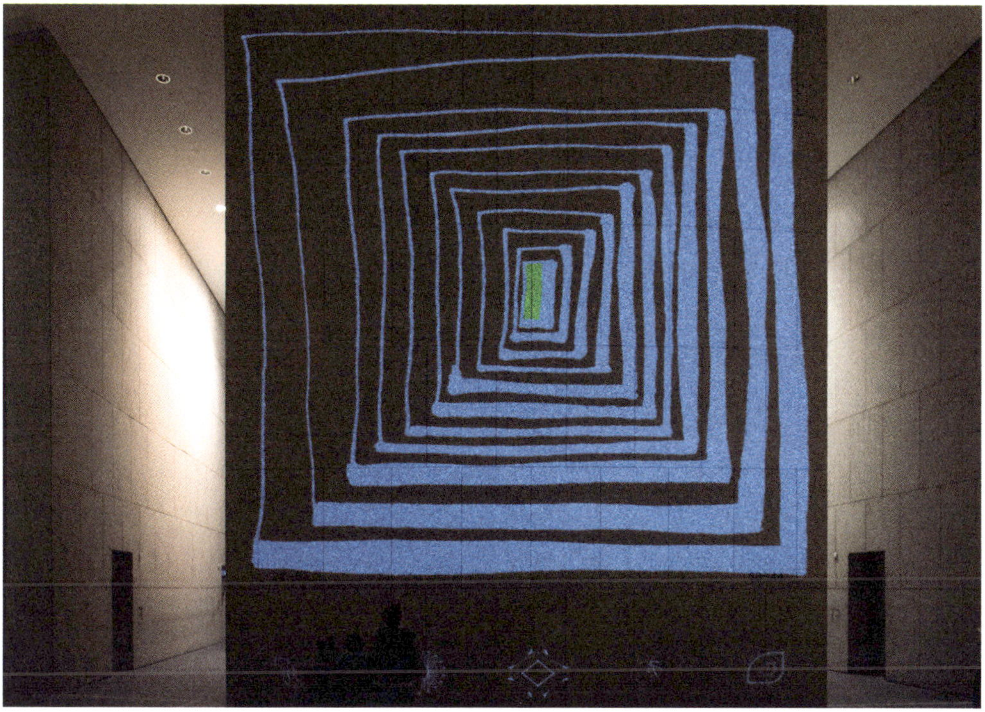

Kate Dunn and Phillip Gough, *Collaborative Mapping*, Grosvenor Place, Photos: Alex Wisser, 2014.

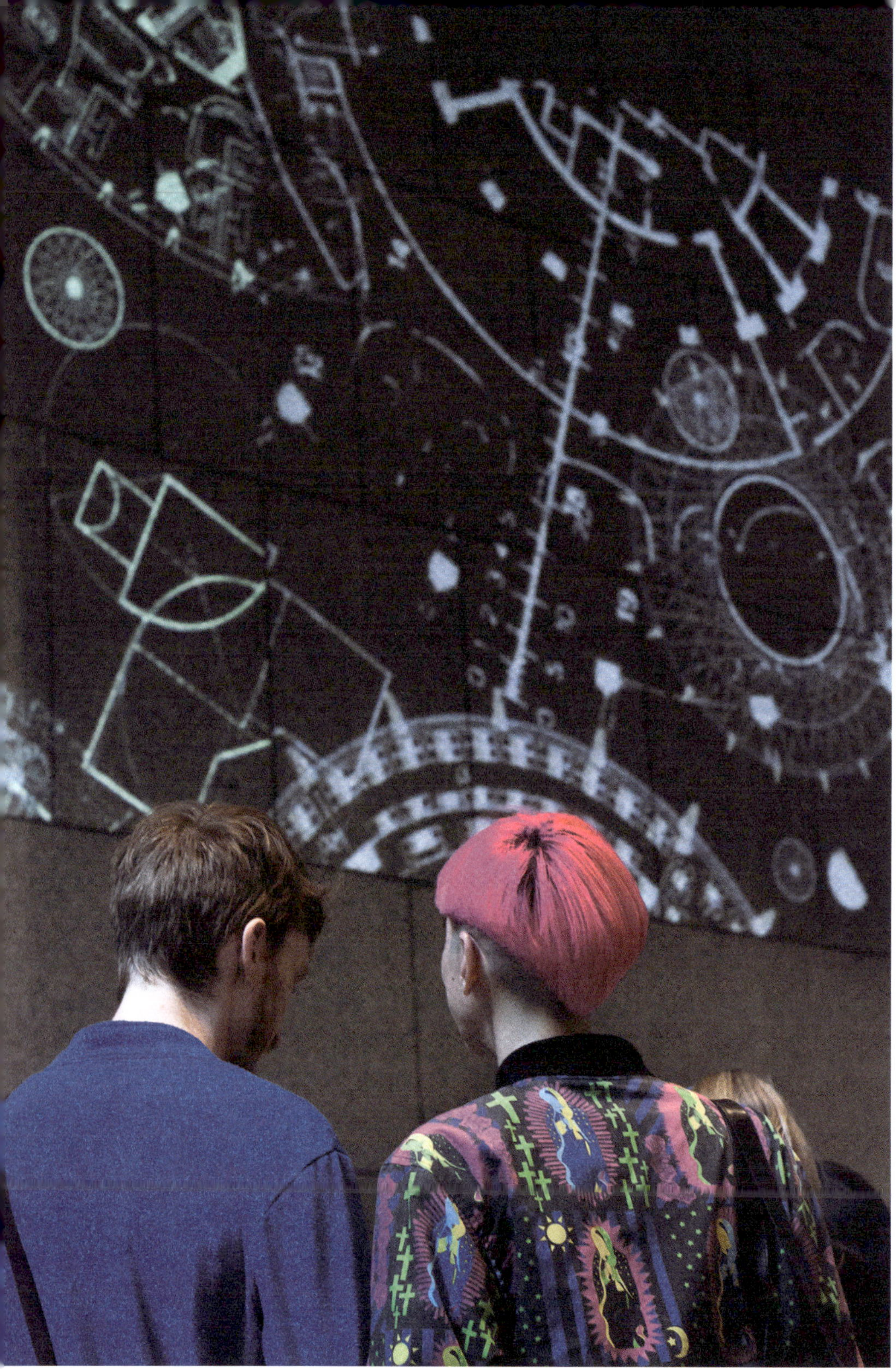

Eduardo Kairuz, *Untitled (Two Powers),* Capita Centre, 9 Castlereagh Street, Photo: Olivia Govan, 2014.

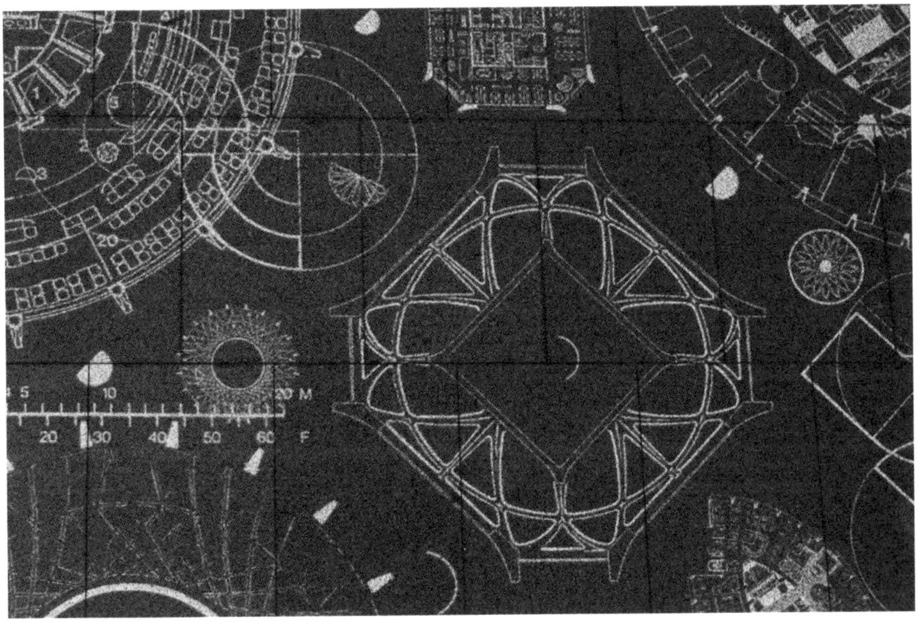

Eduardo Kairuz, *Untitled (Two Powers),* Capita Centre, 9 Castlereagh Street, Photo: Olivia Govan, 2014.

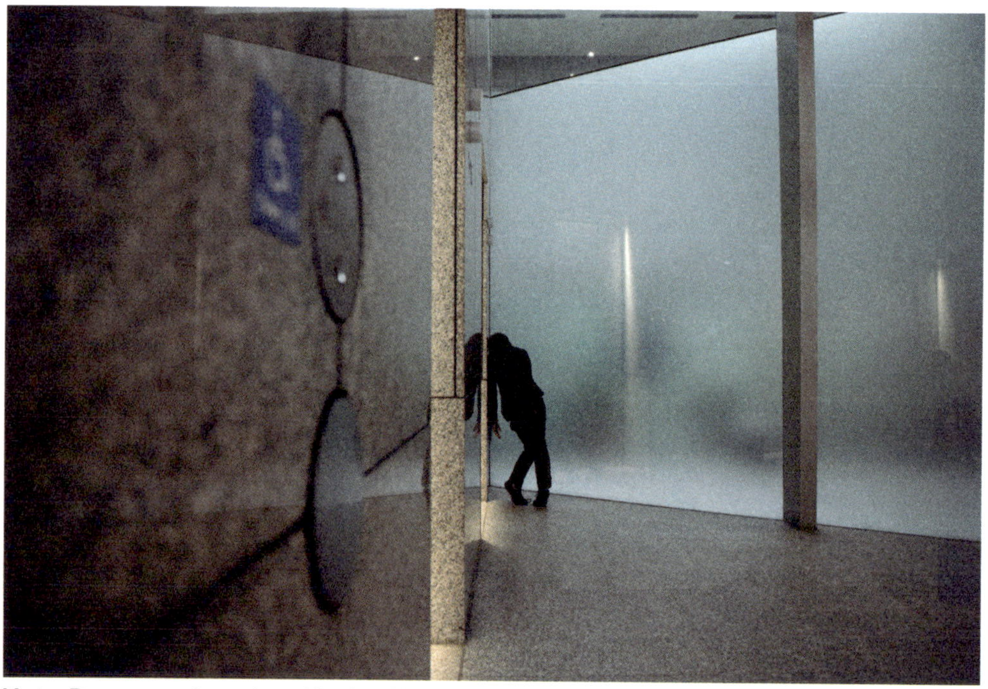

Kate Dunn performing *Under Harry's Circumstances*, Grosvenor Place, Photo: Alex Wisser, 2014.

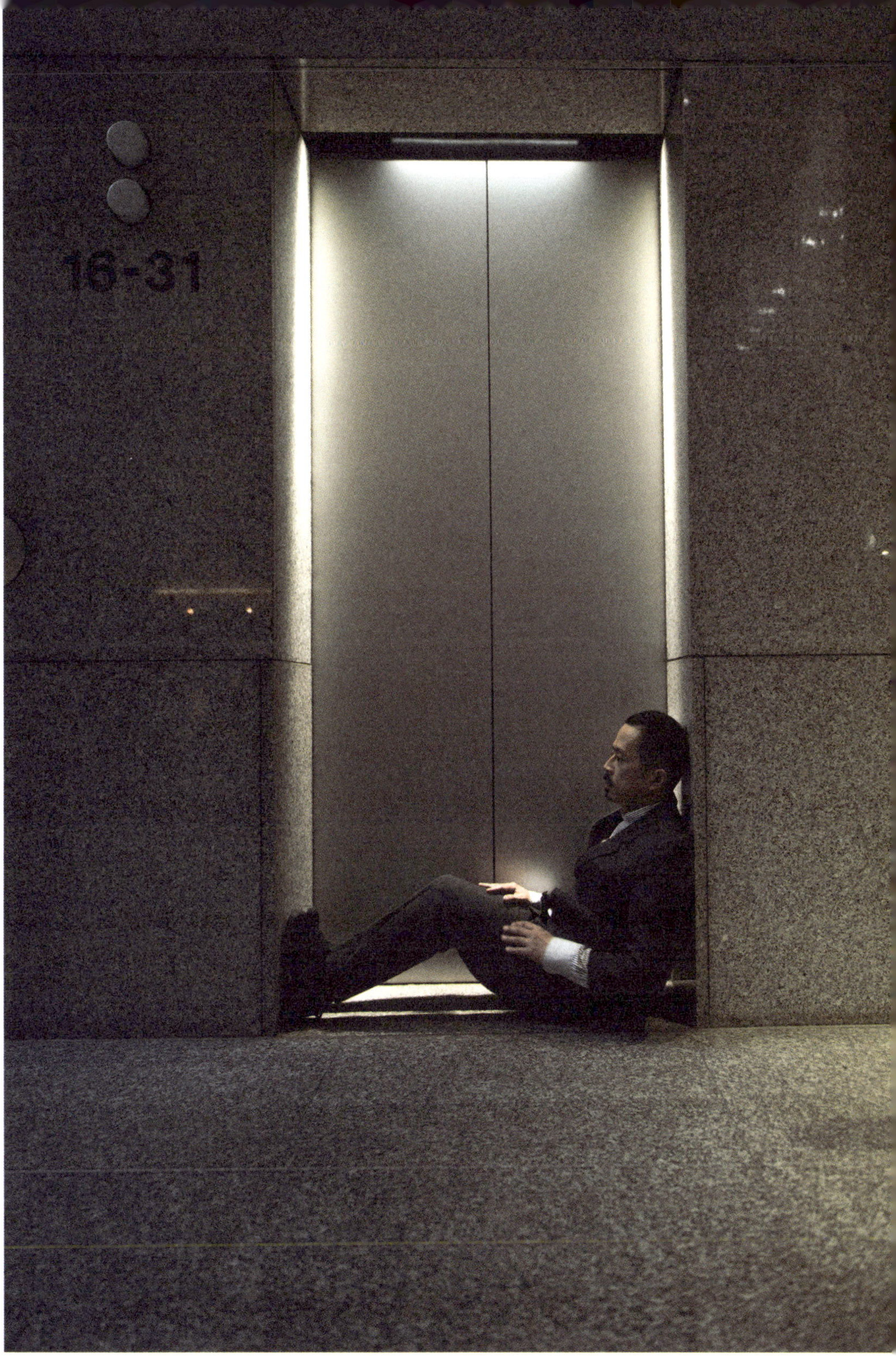

Ryuichi Fujimura performing *Under Harry's Circumstances*, Grosvenor Place, Photo: Alex Wisser, 2014.

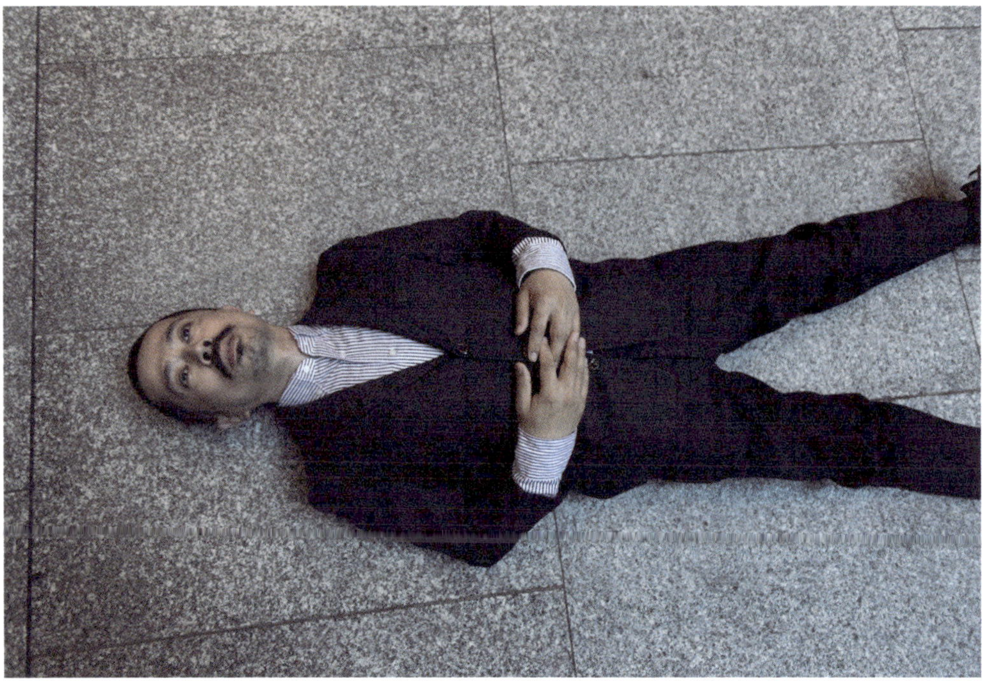

Ryuichi Fujimura performing *Under Harry's Circumstances*, Grosvenor Place, Photo: Alex Wisser, 2014.

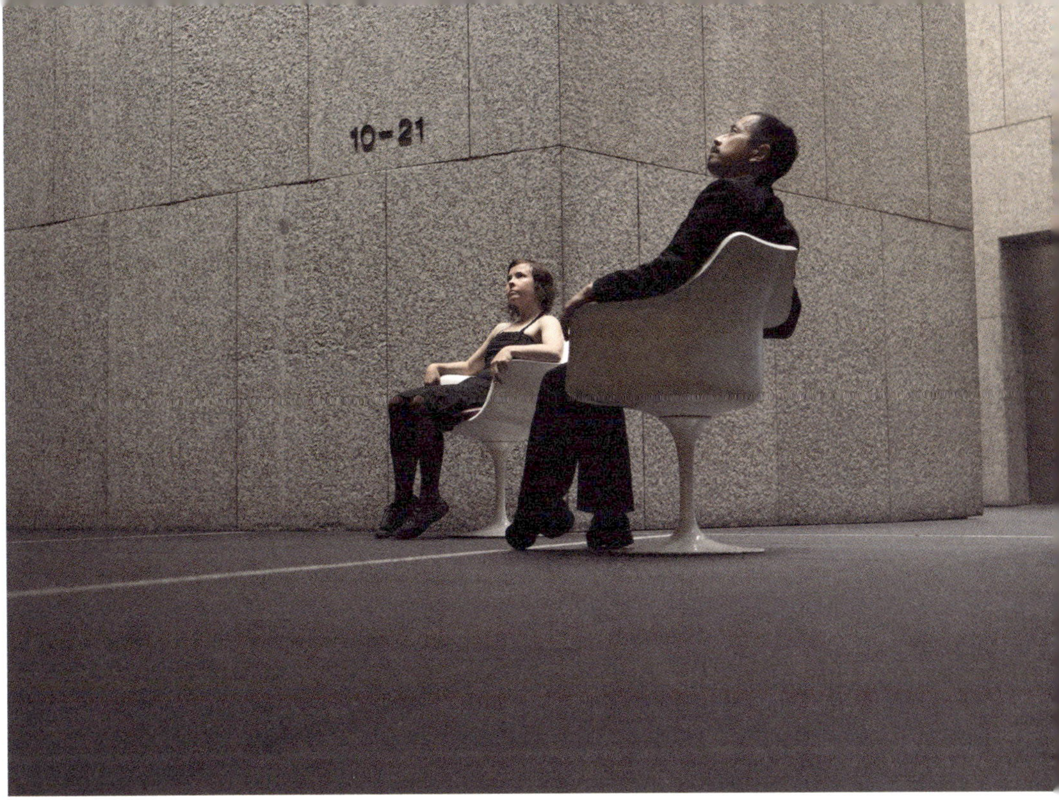

Ryuichi Fujimura and Kate Sherman performing *Under Harry's Circumstances,* Grosvenor Place, Photo: Jung Ming, 2014.

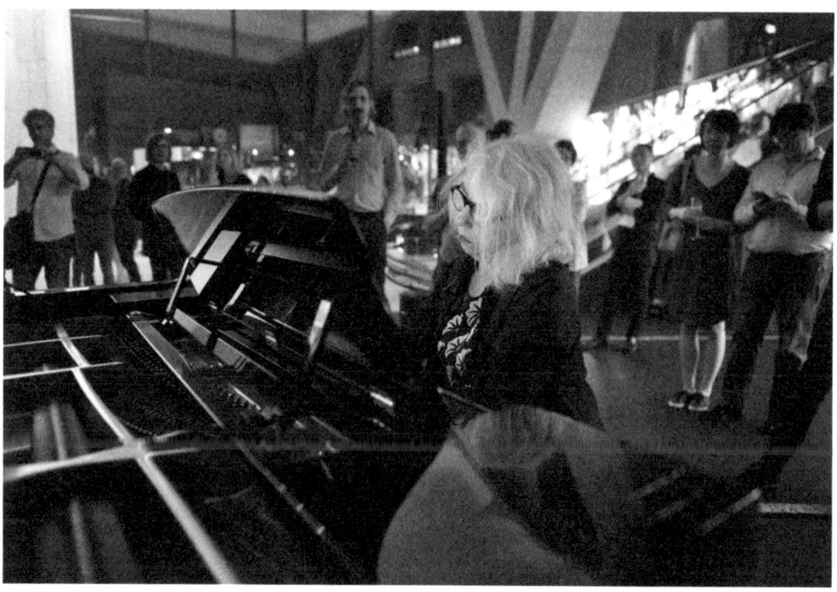

Campbell Drake, Karen Cummings, and Elizabeth Drake,
Temporal Formal: Investigative Spatial Performance,
Elizabeth Drake playing piano, Grosvenor Place,
Photo: Alex Wisser, 2014.

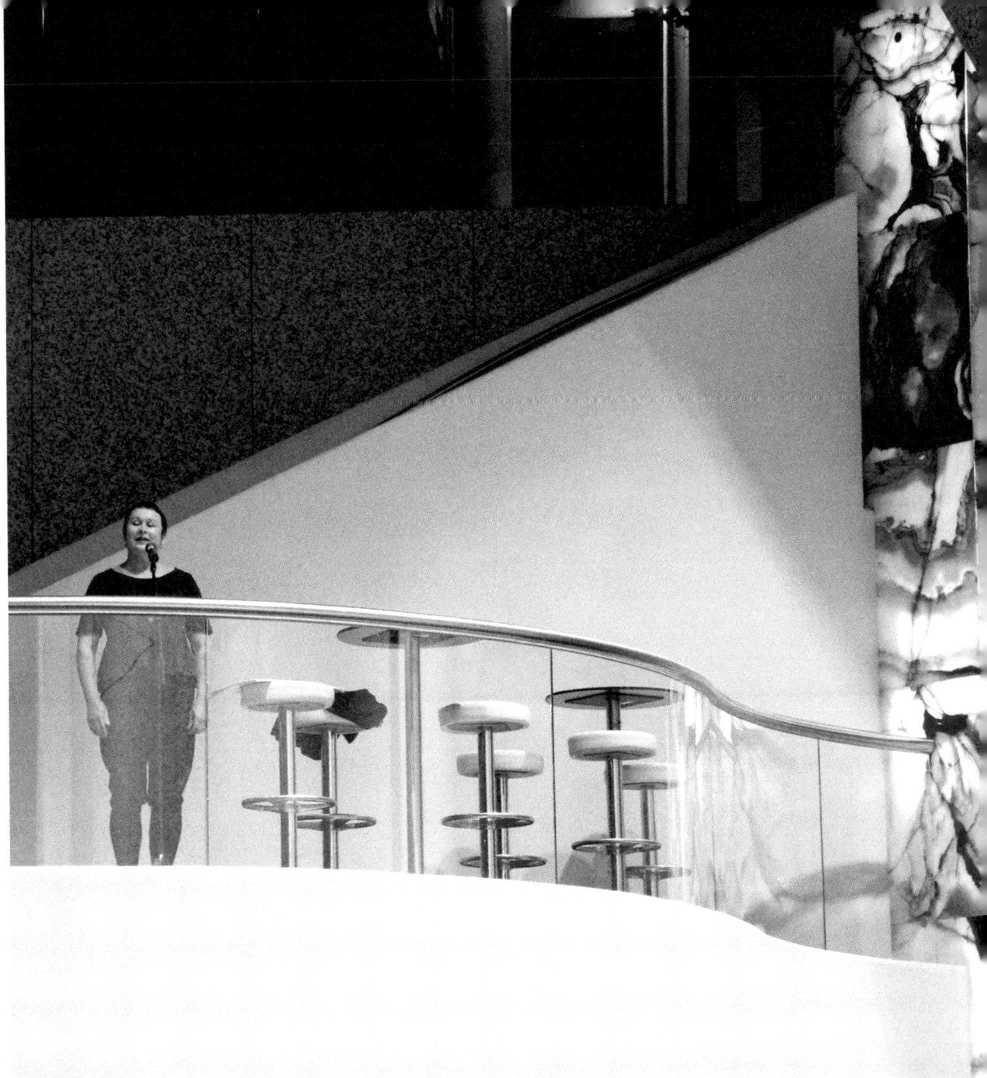

Campbell Drake, Karen Cummings, and Elizabeth Drake,
Temporal Formal: An Investigative Spatial Performance,
Karin Cummings singing, Grosvenor Place,
Photo: Vinchy Yi Wu, 2014.

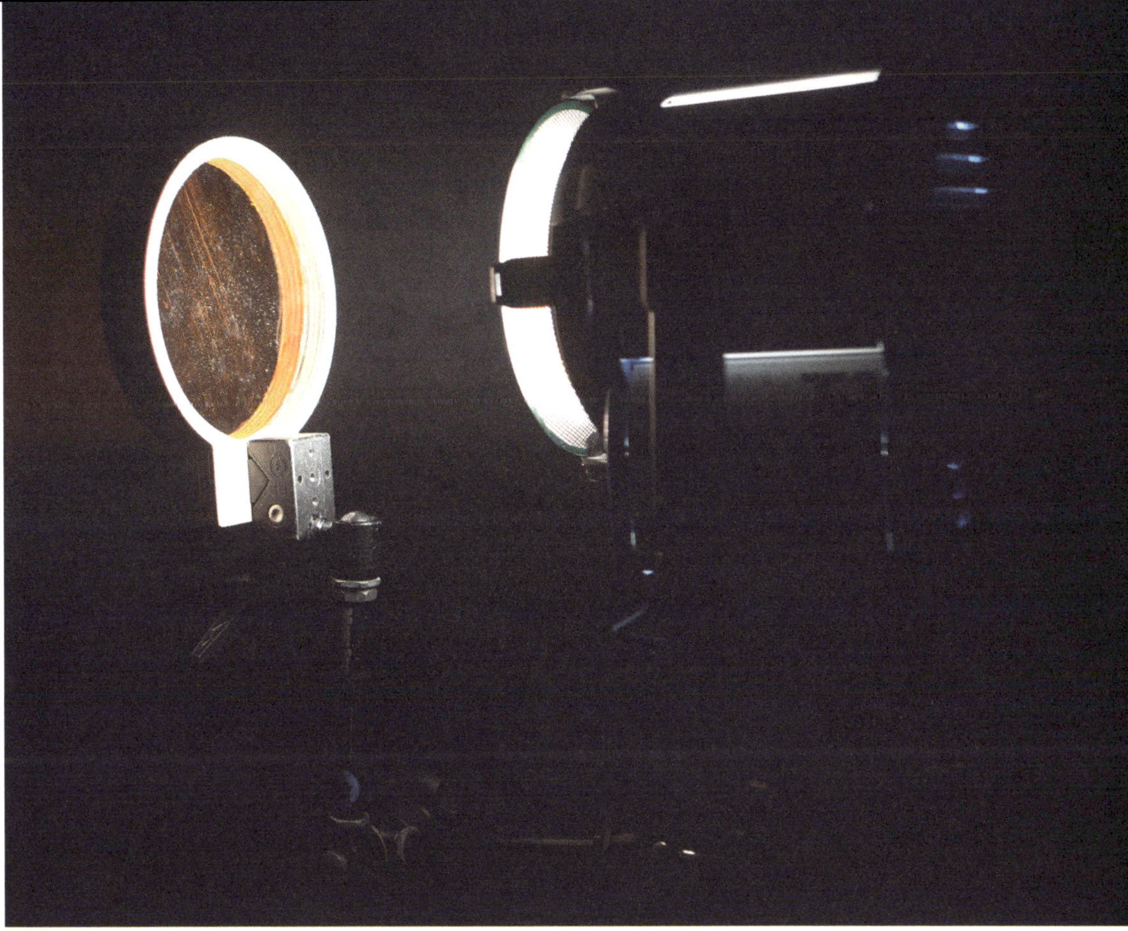

Francis Kenna, *Experiments in Presence,* Grosvenor Place,
Photo: Jung Ming, 2014.

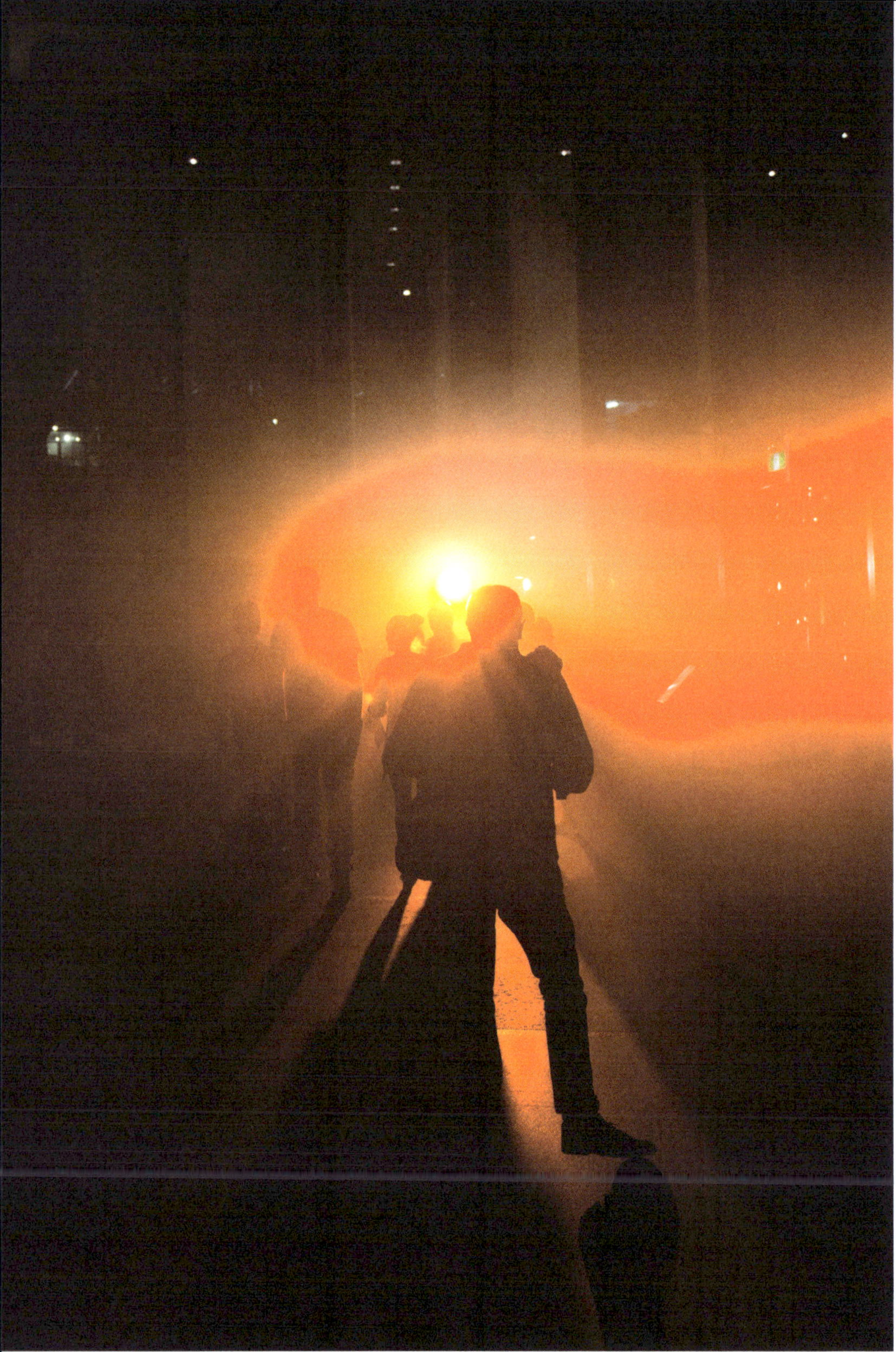

Francis Kenna, *Experiments in Presence,* Grosvenor Place,
Photo: Alex Wisser, 2014.

1 FLOOR PAINTING (p. 81)
Nina and Elena Tory-Henderson

Floor Painting is a direct response to the curved geometry of Harry Seidler's Australia Square. The work consists of a series of large geometric forms of painted carpet on the ground of the external space of the building, radiating outward from the building's edge toward the street. The shapes trace the geometry of the floor plan, connecting the internal space with the public domain. The piece is inspired by the colours and geometry of the Sol LeWitt painting in Australia Square's foyer. Much like LeWitt's wall painting, the carpet becomes part of the architecture and an experiential element to moving through the space.

2 THE MATTER OF VOIDS (pp. 82–85)
Ainslie Murray

The Matter of Voids, a floor-based temporal installation, grew from a quiet obsession with the ceiling in the Australia Square foyer. The ceiling was understood as a repetitious pattern of solid and void. The installation questioned this stark, solid-void duality and investigated the invisible or barely perceived physical matter occupying the void spaces. In doing so, it reconsidered the voids as positive volumes with the capacity to cast a "shadow" upon the floor. Fine particulate matter, a tangible physical component of air and a standard indicator of air quality, was captured and arranged on the floor plane in an intricate geometric pattern that placed the floor in a direct visual dialogue with the ceiling. The installation consisted of two parts separated by an external glass wall. One part was inside the foyer, and the other part continued outside. Inside, areas of finely crushed glass on the floor referenced the voids of the ceiling grid. The glass constituted the particulate matter, a luminous representation of the invisible, suspended matter of the air. Outside, the solids of the ceiling grid were represented by water-soluble embroidery film hand cut to form a geometric "web" with areas of interspersed black silica. During the evening, performance artists Kate Sherman and Ryuichi Fujimura interacted with the installation by spraying a fine mist of water on the film, slowly dissolving the work until it disappeared completely. The work inverted, reversed, and imaginatively multiplied solid and void across the horizontal planes of the building.

3 YOU ARE HEAR (p. 87)
Lindsay Webb and Amanda Cole

You Are Hear is a work of aural architecture, of indoor orienteering for the ears. The sonic environment of Australia Square's tower lobby is microtonally rendered by a detailed geometric analysis of the high, curvilinear ceiling. Twenty discreet, intersecting audio zones corresponding to the ceiling's twenty ribbed, radial segments are composed with precise reference to the geometry of the soffit structure.
The zones are distributed around the outer edge of the ground-level circuit in a modular array of twenty loudspeakers, in between which people move and listen. The spatial approach is a sensory enactment of subjectivity in architecture. As *you* move around the doughnut-shaped foyer, *you are* hearing your precise geolocation within resonating space; tones and rhythms advance and retreat depending on your ambulation; each point sounds like no other spatial point within the foyer; *you are here*. As a formal experiment in sonic

dispersion drawing a direct line from Wassily Kandinsky, Béla Bartók, Arnold Schoenberg, and Iannis Xenakis to Steve Reich and Max Neuhaus, *You Are Hear* works against the traditional presentation of musical scores, wherein patrons receive a work unfolded in time and anchored in a singular space. *You Are Hear* is experienced through exploration. Its entire cubic space is zinging and alive; a comparison can be drawn with undersea animals geolocating via sonic radar. Each loudspeaker's unique palette of (micro)tones is temporally variant, mixing in and out of phase with other speakers to create an ever-evolving performance, and the mobile audience "play the gradient." The piece has the potential for time without end, or more accurately, time until the building's end. On the cyclic temporal-spatial-harmonic map, *you are hear*. We wanted to ask, what are the possibilities of living inside music or a tonal landscape? Can we allow spaces to sound variant and endlessly pleasing by revealing and reveling in their distinct sonic integrity without irritating repetition or overbearing edification? We are attempting to make good on the promise of architecture to behave like a giant musical instrument, through whose effective utilization we might score our lives. We aim to create new kinds of spatial compositions that use the architectural body and its inbuilt electricity to lead us in the construction of positive ambience.

4 HAUS DER FRAU (pp. 88–90)
Cottage Industries

Haus der Frau is a participatory project created for the foyer of Harry Seidler's Australia Square that re-inscribes modernist architecture into the feminized realm of domestic handicraft. The commercial foyer space becomes a temporary craft workshop, as visitors are invited to engage in the production of a large-scale, cross-stitch representation of the building. The structural and aesthetic unity of Seidler's architecture, credited with bringing Bauhaus principles to Australia, is thereby opened to informal play, incompleteness, and error. The title *Haus der Frau* derives from the women's pavilion at the 1914 Deutscher Werkbund exhibition, a model living space reconciling the domestic and professional needs of women. It also alludes to the Bauhaus women's class, which steered females away from "heavy craft" and architecture and toward textiles and weaving. Resisting these constraints, and a workshop master who vowed never to "pick up a thread," the Bauhaus weaving students nevertheless experimented with form, materials, and process. Penelope Seidler's rendering of Blues Point Tower, which transcribes that building's architectural elevation onto the orthogonal grid of cross-stitch, provided a precedent for the current project. In *Haus der Frau*, the distinctive geometry of Australia Square forms the template for a collaborative cross-stitch. A set of tables was custom built with their surfaces etched and perforated according to this template. Visitors to Expanded Architecture were invited to participate in *Haus der Frau* by sewing directly into the tabletops and over the course of the exhibition an image of Australia Square revealed itself in irregular, hand-stitched thread. By inviting visitors to "pick up a thread," *Haus der Frau* explores the contested space between the professionalized spheres of art and architecture and the domestic "pastime" of craft, between the decorative and the functional, and seeks to re-situate the role of women's labour within the Bauhaus and its legacy.

5 TAKE A SEAT (pp. 92–93)
Bellemo & Cat

To celebrate the great modernist work of Harry Seidler, we chose to create a temporary sculptural installation of chairs made by Harry Sebel. The ideals of the Bauhaus led to the design and development of modular furniture, and there was a flourishing in the experimentation of chair design concurrent with mechanization and the modernists' supposed love of the machine era. Quite possibly, the mass production of chairs best epitomizes the modernist ideals of modularity, which although explored in architecture is yet to be fully realized. Although once regarded as subordinate to architecture, the design of furniture, and especially that of chairs, became a separate discipline when its manufacture was transferred from the domain of the craftsman to that of industrial process. Given that this was to be a temporary, "one-night stand" artwork, we chose to create a sculptural piece that not only honours these ideals of rational experimentation, but also does not create more detritus or artwork beyond the memory of it. Hence we rented fifty chairs, choosing one of the more common chairs from the era in which Seidler was most prolific—the Sebel plastic bucket chair. With these we created our installation, a truly temporary artwork that acknowledges its transitory nature. These are the type of chairs that are rented and used for a short period of time. One does not aspire to own or collect them. They are fundamentally utilitarian. To further the cause of modularity, we created a sculptural installation of pieces, or modules, that seem to scuttle across the foyer in an insect-like manner.

6 UNDER HARRY'S CIRCUMSTANCES (pp. 94, 104–107)
Ryuichi Fujimura and Kate Sherman

Under Harry's Circumstances, a thirty-minute dance performance held in all three venues of *Expanded Architecture: Temporal Formal at Seidler City*, brought dance and architecture together based on the Bauhaus idea of creating a total work of art in which all arts, including architecture, would eventually come together. Performing the same choreography of set movement phrases and improvisational scores at Australia Square, Capita Centre, now 9 Castlereagh Street, and Grosvenor Place allowed the work to be informed and trans-formed by each environment, examining how time, space, and place inform meaning. Part of the choreographic process for this work involved research into the extensive history of the three buildings, including collecting current and past images, as well as literature on them, and visiting the three locations to observe the inhabitants of the sites and spaces. The process also incorporated such references as Oskar Schlemmer's Das Triadische Ballett, an iconic dance piece of the Bauhaus era. *Under Harry's Circumstances* investigates our relationship with our surroundings, how our environments inform us, and how meaning is changed by circumstance and context. The performance at 9 Castlereagh Street included original music by the UK-based composer Grace Huie Robbins.

7 SENTRIES (pp. 96–97)
Tina Fox

The three existing small square granite plinths outside the entrance to 9 Castlereagh Street were extruded upwards, with string and crochet to create temporary soft, tall columns. Their rectilinear form and graphic black and white patterning borrow directly from the modular, formal art of the 1960s and the striking tiled mural by Lin Utzon in the lobby of Capita Centre, now 9 Castlereagh Street.

The work was also influenced by the minimalist, repetitive, graphic, and architectural nature of works by the artist Sol LeWitt and the functional aesthetic of Harry Seidler. *Sentries,* however, presents a more domesticated version of minimalism through its hand-crafted style, slight irregularity, and soft surfaces. Softness tends to be viewed as an undesirable character trait, but in this work it offers an interesting contrast to the architecture around it. The crochet itself becomes undomesticated, situated in a corporate environment, but brings with it hints of home. It begs to be touched and hugged, demanding an emotional, human connection. Columns have feelings too.

As a trained architect and contemporary artist, I am always interested in blending ideas from architecture, art, and craft together to reinterpret and challenge our preconceptions of the built environment. *Sentries* stands silently and watches busy people marching in and out of the building. The plinths have acquired personality. What are they thinking? Are they benevolent, waiting for a hug, or are they judging the fast-paced world around them?

8 COLLABORATIVE MAPPING (pp. 99–101)
Kate Dunn and Phillip Gough

The 2014 Expanded Architecture project *Collaborative Mapping* emerged from a series of collaborative projects (replete with hurdles, successes, and failures) into a series of large-scale interactive projected images developed over a period of six weeks. The projected images incorporate some of the significant motifs and forms repeatedly found in Harry Seidler's buildings as well as the motifs of the artists who inspired him and with whom he collaborated.

The original proposal used the floor at the entrance to Australia Square as a projection surface, with people interacting with the work by traversing the screening area. The projection would alter and transform as people moved through the space, generating new geometric forms. It was initially proposed to visually map the collaboration between Seidler and the artists with whom he worked, but it soon became apparent that this would be difficult, as accurate records of the exact nature of their exchanges and collaboration do not exist.

To document the process of collaboration, the artists created a diary of *Collaborative Mapping*'s development. The diary documents the creation of a series of boundary objects designed to facilitate effective communication between the practitioners from somewhat similar backgrounds and creative environments. In 1989 Susan Star and James Greisemer had introduced the concept of boundary objects to define and describe objects that have different meanings to different social groups. They used a map as an example of a boundary object that facilitates communication and collaboration. One does not need to be a cartographer to read a map, but once the "language" of maps has been learned, a map can be read by anyone.

The language used in the arts is quite different from that of information visualization. Examples of the hindrances to communication between us on ideas and methodologies include language, different visual cues, and lack of knowledge in the other person's area of expertise. To overcome these hindrances, a range of boundary objects was developed using iterative design strategies. We employed such techniques as sketching and the diary documenting and reflecting on the process and test projections. Engaging in this collaboration illuminated our knowledge boundaries, generated new ways of working, and facilitated the fabrication of artworks. Inspiration from Seidler's collaboration with a wide range of artists, the interactive work created, and the iterative process used to make the work brought about new understandings of the conditions necessary for effective collaboration and the creation of new artworks.

9 UNTITLED (pp. 102–103) (TWO POWERS)

Eduardo Kairuz

Le Corbusier, in his seminal book of 1923, *Toward an Architecture*, famously proclaims not once, but twice, "The house is a machine for living in." Responding to the provocation of this edition of Expanded Architecture and the enormous influence Le Corbusier had on Harry Seidler's work, *Untitled (Two Powers)* seeks to reclaim and rework the Swiss-French architect's seminal quotation. Through the extraction, edition, and animation of technical drawings for Australia Square and the MLC Centre, *Untitled (Two Powers)*—the title paraphrasing *Two Towers*, a 1980 Phillip Drew publication about these two iconic buildings—presents the towers combined as a faulty clockwork mechanism. In the work, Seidler's drawings come alive, with the radial and concentric compositions transformed into rotating gears, cogwheels, and pistons.

The installation was also influenced by *Mechanical Principles*, a short film from 1930 by the American filmmaker and photographer Ralph Steiner depicting carefully choreographed close-ups of machines and mechanisms in hypnotizing, continuous motion.

Untitled (Two Powers) explores the intersection between film and architecture in the form of a two-channel, silent video installation in which two fundamental means of architecture—drawing and orthogonal projection—are subordinated to two fundamental elements of film—time and movement. Thus cinema—the medium of modernity par excellence, where time, space, and movement are collapsed into complex units thanks to the use of various machines—becomes an instrument to liberate architecture from one of its most notorious conditions: the inability to move. Also, the work brings to attention new connections between Seidler's architecture and the ambitions (and failures) of the modernist ideal.

The result is a visual architectural machine in erroneous and perpetual motion—an even more abstract representation of architecture that challenges its heroic ambitions, inertia, and permanence.

10 TEMPORAL FORMAL: (pp. 108–109)
AN INVESTIGATIVE SPATIAL PERFORMANCE
Campbell Drake, Karen Cummings, and Elizabeth Drake

> The architecture allowed for the performances to take place. It created the various circumstances for the performances to take place. Acoustically, visually, aesthetically, socially, it also created part of the performance.
> — Audience member

Adopting piano and voice as temporal and transient mediums, *Temporal Formal* is an investigative spatial performance that explores intersections between music, architecture, and history. Drawing inspiration from "24 Hours John Cage," an event staged at Bauhaus Dessau in 2012, the piece features the performance of a selection of works by influential composers drawn from and inspired by the Bauhaus era. It begins with Elizabeth Drake performing Arnold Schoenberg's *Six Little Piano Pieces,* op. 19, a solo offering a musical parallel to the modernist project of the Bauhaus in the form of twelve-tone music. Following the Schoenberg composition, Drake and Karen Cummings perform selections from *Songs from Liquid Days,* by Phillip Glass. The songs were first performed in 1986, the year in which construction began on Grosvenor Place. Composed for piano and voice, this part of the performance offers an extension and counterpoint to Schoenberg's twelve-tone music in the form of minimalist music. It is structured through repetitive blocks or modules, producing a playful monumentality via small shifts between blocks.

The patterning and repetition employed in *Songs from Liquid Days* provides an aesthetic resemblance to the geometries and patterns Harry Seidler chose for Grosvenor Place. According to music critic Stephen Holden, *Songs from Liquid Days* are short, oracular reflections with imagery that explicitly evokes mystical connections between people and objects. To extend this connection between people and architecture, the audience, onlookers, and Grosvenor Place residents were invited to sit, move around, or pass through the performance.

> I feel the music, as a performance, activated a social space. As such, the building became responsive to people and performances. The operatic performance was well suited to the scale of the foyer and in many ways tied all the artworks together.
> — Audience member 01

The operatic programming within the public foyer of an office tower offers an opportunity to engage and reposition public perception via the re-appropriation of commercial space. Through the musical renditions of Schoenberg and Glass, *Temporal Formal* asks the audience to make connections between music, history, and the surrounding architecture. Allowing one to experience the performance and the architectural environment simultaneously, this Bauhaus-styled happening provides an immersive moment in which a heightened spatial awareness provokes the forging of new relationships between the immediate environment, performance, and the social-cultural and historical contexts of site and place.

11 EXPERIMENTS IN PRESENCE (pp. 111–112)

Francis Kenna

> Thus we cannot remain in a single viewpoint, we need more for the sake of free vision.
> — Josef Albers, *Despite Straight Lines*

Presence emerges in quiet reflection, a fluid moment between subject and object. The spatial investigations of Edmund Husserl and the perceptual experiments of Josef Albers touch on the idea of presence. Over time, these influences have more than any other shaped my ideas and practice as an artist. Following these influences, I performed an experiment in spatial perception, filling the foyer of Grosvenor Place with thick, orange fog.

Husserl defines pure phenomenology as the investigation of pure phenomena, a science of the immediate objects of experience.

Phenomenology fundamentally concerns the relationship between subject and object, "an 'object' being taken purely as something having just those determinations with which it presents itself in consciousness and in just those changing modes through which it presents itself."[1] Following this, Albers' art can be placed firmly within the field of phenomenology as defined by Husserl, quite literally testing the phenomena of spatial perception and duration. As colours shift and lines dance before our eyes, the viewer's mutable experience becomes central to the work. These experiments blur the boundaries between subject and object. Changes in perspective are stretched over time as solid volumes become empty and voids are filled, softly shattering the objectivity of our everyday experience of space.

Perhaps the most striking comparison between Albers and Husserl is in the way they both questioned static notion's objecthood. For Husserl, the object has no form of its own—at least, not in the physical sense that we know it—but is rather co-produced by us and our cognitive, form-giving processes. Our perceptions are in a constant state of change, forming a flood of raw sensation seamlessly entering and altering the stream of consciousness. By making explicit the duration contained within the act of seeing, Albers' art constitutes a kind of experiment in perceptual presentation as distinct from representation. In other words, it is an experiment in presence. My experiment was an attempt to recontextualize Grosvenor Place as a site for temporal engagement. Through the active engagement of the viewer, the orange fog breaks through the habitual shell of everyday experience and allows a temporal experience to emerge. The work activates a conditional situation, enabling subjective, embodied engagement with the site. This conditional relationship is grounded in the subjective modes of spatial experience, challenging the rationalization of re-presentational space. Thus, the objective of these experiments is the reintroduction of time to our understanding of objects. By acknowledging the contingency of space in perceptual and social contexts, we can begin to break down the static idea of space in favour of a more temporal exchange with presence.

1 Edmund Husserl, "Pure Phenomenology, Its Method, and Its Field of Investigation," in *Husserl's Shorter Works*, ed. Peter McCormick and Frederick Elliston (Brighton, 1981), p. 132.

IV

UNSTABLE ARCHITECTURES; OR CAMPING, MODERNISM, AND BEYOND

Thea Brejzek and Lawrence Wallen

> The nomad is not necessarily someone who moves:
> there are travels in which one does not move,
> travels in intensity, ... nomads (are) those who start
> nomadizing in order to stay in the same place
> and free themselves from codes.
> — Gilles Deleuze, "Nomad Thought"

In architecture as much as in philosophical thought, temporary occupations have offered an alternative vision of inhabitation to the constraints of a society that typically defines itself through conventions of settledness, stability, and duration. Gilles Deleuze's notion of nomadism as an activity and a process that creates a counterspace to the dominant space of the state provides one set of relations with which to think about temporal and transient built structures and contemporary reflections.[1] Heidegger's idea of "dwelling" as a mode of "being in the world," where identity is not linked to a place, forms another theoretical provocation.

1 Gilles Deleuze, "Nomad Thought," in *The New Nietzsche: Contemporary Styles of Interpretation*, ed. David B. Allison (Cambridge, 1999).

The phenomenon of "transience" in modernist architecture and postmodernist transdisciplinary and architectural experimentation are examined here in case studies spanning 1922 to 2012 that have a common origin in the positively connoted notion of the nomadic—the temporary and unsettled. Two of the case studies are modernist examples of "unstable architectures"—Rudolph Schindler's Kings Road House (1922) in Los Angeles and Eileen Gray's E1027 (1926–29) in Roquebrune-Cap-Martin—allow reflection on the architects' desire for the design of their own houses as distinctly temporal dwellings. In contrast, the third case study, Marathon Camp (2012), designed and built some 60 years later by the architect collective raumlaborberlin at the Steirischer Herbst Festival in Graz, Austria, represents not a private dwelling, but a model for the temporary housing of "theory," that is, for localized and collective thinking. The concept of unstable architectures, it is argued, is linked to the creation of systems of performative relations between people and spaces through experimentation, critique, and contextualization. Unstable architectures provoke and enable alternate modes of individual and collective behavior, and in doing so, these built structures serve to destabilize and unsettle existing social orders.

Kings Road House, Los Angeles

The "origin and driving force of modernity" is how the anthropologist and geographer David Harvey describes Baudelaire's definition of modernity from the French writer's essay "The Painter of Modern Life" (1863). Baudelaire wrote, "Modernity is the transient, the fleeting, the contingent; it is the one-half of art, the other being the eternal and the immutable."[2] In this short excerpt, Baudelaire links modernity to the temporal and fleeting as much as to that which is unchangeable. The dichotomy of the two conditions may be seen as a result of the weakening and dissolving of the singularly driven project of the Enlightenment that enables the conflicting ambitions of modernity. Modernist architecture, however, Harvey argues, has looked upon the city as the singular object of the master plan, whereas postmodernism understands space to be distributed and autonomous.[3]

The work of the architect Rudolph Schindler (1887–1953), an Austrian émigré, embodies a notion of the temporal and transitory that may seem to be at odds with the notion of the urban master plan, while at the same time unwaveringly adhering to "shelter" as architecture's origin and centerpiece. As a student of Otto Wagner in Vienna and influenced by Adolf Loos' *Raumplan,* the highly differentiated spatial organization of the interior that Loos refers to as the three-dimensional rendering of a ground plan, Schindler left Vienna in 1914 hoping to work for Frank Lloyd Wright, whose radical work he had seen in the 1910 portfolio published by Ernst Wasmuth.[4] Schindler began working for Wright in 1918, running his American office while Wright worked on the Imperial Hotel in Tokyo. In 1920, Wright sent him to Los Angeles to supervise construction of the Hollyhock House for the oil heiress Aline Barnsdall.

In 1921 Schindler and his wife, Pauline, went on a camping trip to Yosemite National Park. For Schindler, immersion in the Californian wilderness became a social and architectural programme, and within weeks after the Yosemite trip, he found a site on which to build his private home. The house was designed during November and December 1921, with construction beginning on the West Hollywood site in early 1922 (Fig. 1). Schindler called the design a "permanent camp,"[5] while one observer referred to it as a "glorified tent."[6]

Schindler's work stands for architectural solutions that mediate seamlessly between the "grounded" and the "infinite," bearing an echo of Heidegger's concept of the fourfold that is both part of our being in space and part of dwelling.[7] At the same time, Heidegger's notion of shelter does not refer to a stable identity through site. Mark Wigley writes in favour of a reevaluation of Heidegger's concept of house as one that comprises "a nomadic, displaced frame of reference," in line with Heidegger's notion of "dwelling as an activity" and "dwelling is thinking."[8] Space therefore emerges from place and is realized through the fourfold. It is thus that space is created prior to experience.

2 David Harvey, *The Condition of Postmodernity* (Cambridge, Mass. 1983), p. 10.

3 Ibid., 66–98.

4 *Ausgeführte Bauten und Entwürfe von Frank Lloyd Wright* (Berlin, 1910), featuring 100 lithographs of works by Frank Lloyd Wright.

5 MAK Center for Art and Architecture, Schindler House and Studio, Los Angeles, http://makcenter.org.

6 Leisa Zeigler, "California Moderne," *ICON: World Monuments Fund,* Spring 2003, p. 41, http://www.wmf.org/dig-deeper/article/california-moderne.

7 "In saving the earth, in receiving the sky, in awaiting the divinities, in initiating mortals, dwelling occurs as the fourfold preservation of the fourfold. To spare and preserve means: to take under our care, to look after the fourfold in its presencing. What we take under our care must be kept safe. But if dwelling preserves the fourfold, where does it keep the fourfold's nature? How do mortals make their dwelling such a preserving? Mortals would never be capable of it if dwelling were merely a staying on earth under the sky, before the divinities, among mortals. Rather, dwelling itself is always a staying with things. Dwelling, as preserving, keeps the fourfold in that with which mortals stay: in things." Martin Heidegger, "Building Dwelling Thinking," in *Poetry, Language, Thought*, trans. Albert Hofstadter (New York, 1971), p. 4.

8 Mark Wigley, "Conceptual Caretakers," in *Territorial Investigations,* ed. Annette W. Baklava and Henk Slager (Amsterdam, 1999), p. 176.

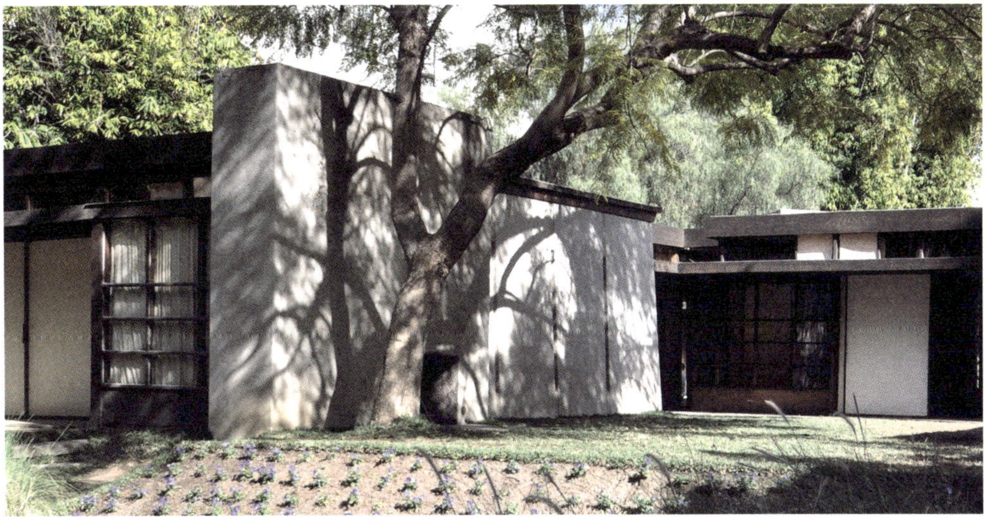

Fig. 1 Rudolph Schindler, *Kings Road House*, Los Angeles, 1922, looking west, Photo: Desley Luscombe, date unknown.

In 1912, while still in Vienna, Schindler, the nomad-architect, had written a manifesto in which he declared, "The architect has finally discovered the medium of his art: space."[9] Indeed, Schindler referred to himself as a space architect and developed and utilized a modular construction system within an architectural programme that he called a "space reference frame," with a basic unit of four feet. In 1946 he wrote in the American journal *Architect and Engineer,*

> To the space architect, however, a proper unit system is essential. He must establish a unit system which he can easily carry in his mind and which will give him the size values of his forms. ... In order to be useful, the unit must have a simple relation to human stature and must be large enough to keep the necessary number of units required to size the average room small enough for easy grasp. It must be small enough to Ž fill all needs for detail sizes by sub-dividing into simple fractions which can be easily pictured 1/2, 1/3, 1/4 at the most.[10]

The Kings Road House, or the Schindler House as it is known today, is located at 835 Kings Road, in West Hollywood. It is positioned at the intersection of a transient and a fixed architectural programme. With a clearly demarcated building structure of copper panels, redwood frames, and tilt slab concrete construction, it intriguingly incorporates spaces with no definitive purpose. Built for two couples, the Schindlers and their friends Clyde and Marian Chace,[11] there are no designated bedrooms. Instead, "sleeping baskets" are perched on top of the building, because Schindler thought the mild

9 David Gebhard, ed., *The Architectural Drawings of R. M. Schindler* (Santa Barbara, 1993), p. 35.

10 Patricia Kucker, "Framework: Construction and Space in the Architecture of Frank Lloyd Wright and Rudolf Schindler," *Journal of Architecture* 7 (Summer 2002): 171–90; Rudolph Schindler, "Reference Frames in Space," *Architect and Engineer,* April 1946, pp. 10, 40, 42–43.

11 In 1924 the Chaces moved to Florida, and the living arrangement shifted, as part of the house was rented to, among others the actor George O'Hara and the composer John Cage. In 1925 the architect Richard Neutra and his wife, Dione, moved in for a number of years. Neutra and Schindler collaborated during this period and made a significant contribution to what came to be known as Californian modernism.

Californian climate would allow for sleeping outdoors. Open fireplaces, inside the house and outside, inscribe the notion of the campfire in the modernist house, and a communal kitchen completes Schindler's vision of a way of living in which each space is open to definition by its inhabitants and where architecture lets go of the dominating force of material mass (Fig. 2).

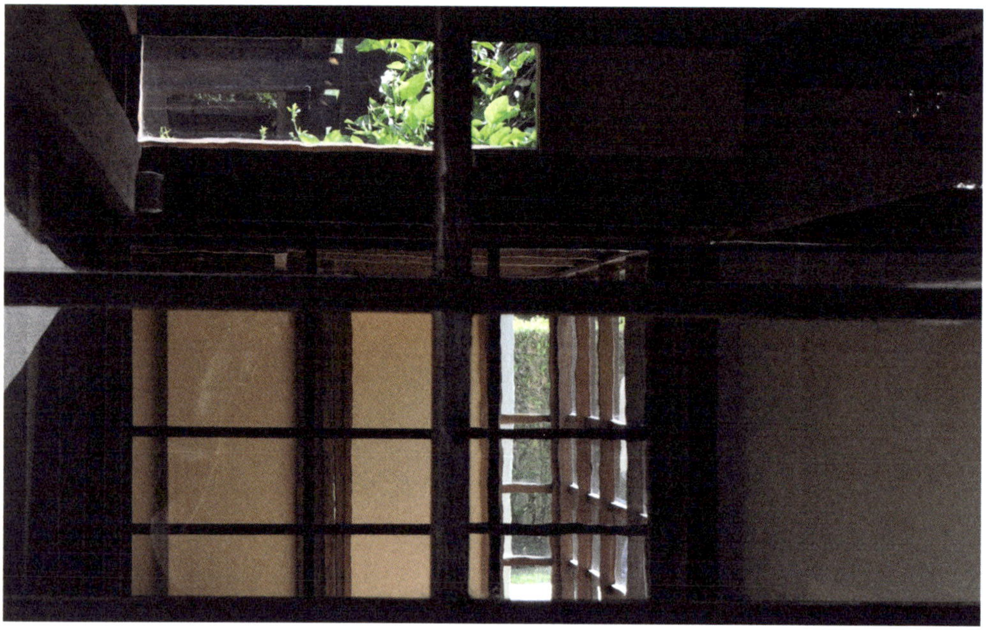

Fig. 2 Rudolph Schindler, *Kings Road House*, 1922, interior view, Photo: Desley Luscombe, date unknown.

> We no longer have plastically shaped material-mass. ... The only idea is space (*Raum*) and its organization. Lacking material-mass, the negative interior space (*Raum*) appears positively on the exterior of the house. Thus the "box-shaped house" has appeared as the primitive form of this new line of development.[12]

Interior partitions can be removed to accommodate more people, and rather than designated bedrooms and living and dining rooms, four studios were created, one for each member of the small community. Furniture was easily moved, and spaces not pre-designated were understood as voids to be assigned meaning as desired. Right before his death, Schindler reflected on the origins of the house, stating,

> When I first came to live & work in California, I camped under the redwood, on the beach, the foothills & the desert. I tested its adobe, its granite & its sky. And out of a carefully built up conception of how the human being could grow roots in this soil—unique & delightful—I built my house.[13]

12 Lionel March and Judith Sheine, eds., *R. M. Schindler: Composition and Construction* (London, 1993), p. 10.

13 Susan Morgan, "Being There: Esther McCoy, the Accidental Architectural Historian," *Archives of American Art Journal* 48, nos. 1–2 (2009): 19.

Schindler also wrote, "The distinction between the indoors and out-of-doors will disappear. The walls will be few, thin and removable. All rooms will become part of an organic unit, instead of being small separate boxes with peepholes."[14] While the spaces for each of the four adults are of equal hierarchy and ungendered, they are spatially distinct in the manner in which the interior seamlessly flows into the exterior, and the open fireplaces inside and outside the house operate as central points of congregation. These are, however, scattered rather than concentrated in a central location. It is this premise, based on the dual notions of impermanence and belonging articulated through architectural form, that differentiates the Kings Road House from other modernist projects of the time and reminds one of Deleuze's topographical concept of smooth versus striated space as a complex pairing of both the nomadic and the sedentary human impetus and the constant interplay between them.

14 August Sarnitz, *R. M. Schindler: Architect, 1887–1953* (New York, 1988), p. 386.

E1027, Roquebrune-Cap-Martin

At the same time Schindler was building his house on Kings Road, the successful Irish interior and furniture designer Eileen Gray (1878–1976) was expanding her practice into architecture. Some of her furniture had been included in the *Salon d'Automne* (1922), along with architectural projects by Le Corbusier (1887–1965) and Robert Mallet-Stevens (1886–1945). Encouraged by Jean Badovici, her partner and the architect and editor of *L'Architecture Vivante* (1923–33), Gray began working on hypothetical architectural projects that led to the design and construction of her holiday home, the E1027 villa (1924–29) at Roquebrune-Cap-Martin, in the south of France, in collaboration with Badovici.

In 1898 Gray had begun studying painting and drawing, first at the Slade School of Fine Art in London followed by further studies from 1901 to 1905 at the Académie Julian and the École Colarossi in Paris. On her return to London from Paris in 1905, she became fascinated with decorative lacquer work, and upon returning to Paris in 1907, she spent a number of years working and perfecting the art of lacquer under the guidance of a young lacquerer, Seizo Sugawara, from Jahoji in northern Japan. At the onset of World War I, she moved back to London with Sugawara and then returned to Paris in 1917, after the war had ended.

Between 1917 and 1921, Gray was commissioned to design and realize the interior, furnishings, and furniture of an apartment for Madame Mathieu Lévy on the rue de Lota in Paris. It was for this single commission that some of here most famous pieces of furniture were created, including the Bibendum Chair, the Serpent Chair, the lacquered Block Screen, and the Pirogue Boat Bed. The project also served to highlight her innovative approach to material and its influence on her perception of space. Through her lacquered panels, furniture, and furnishings, Gray devised "a unified, functional and abstract proposal that was essentially modern yet evidently contained a certain respect for the old. ... The overall effect of these contrasts was to create a cohesive whole."[15] The project was well received by the press and served as a platform for critical interest in her work, with it and other projects being published in various journals, including *L'Architecture Vivante, L'Architecture d'Aujourd'hui, Der Baumeister, Les Cahiers d'Art, L'Arredamento Moderno,* and *Wendingen*.

Gray shifted her practice over the years, moving from painting to lacquer ware to lacquered furniture, woven rugs to interior design, and finally into architecture, assimilating components of each discipline and integrating them in this way. As Caroline Constant wrote, "She never isolated the individual element or made it represent the totality of the ensemble. The result is a richly realized totality of space."[16] On returning from an influential and productive trip to the deserts of North Africa, and bolstered by the critical success of her rue de Lota project, Gray opened Galerie Jean Desert in 1922 as a small shop at 217 rue du Faubourg Saint-Honoré. It remained in operation until 1930. During this period, she began developing her architectural projects. Although early influences may have included the Scottish art nouveau architect Charles Rennie Mackintosh (1868–1928), her architectural projects were clearly grounded in the aesthetics of the architectural avant-garde of the time, including the pivotal modernist architects Auguste Perret (1874–1954), Mallet-Stevens, and Le Corbusier.

Her design for furniture shifted away from lacquered surfaces to chrome and steel frames, developing a "furniture type for the house, which she termed 'le style camping.' These items are flexible, light and portable, capable of assuming different configurations to accommodate a range of activities."[17] With E1027, Gray posited a counter-position to the rapid acceleration of life during the period between the two world wars. Parallel to unprecedented urbanization, leisure camps, vacation centers, and weekend cities had emerged, and Gray had participated in the design of these new conglomerates. Her main concern, however, remained how to overcome the increasingly undifferentiated blurring between private and public life. Even if the camping method suppressed the unfolding of an inner life, Gray tried to link interiority in the private zones of E1027's private spaces, although they mostly were open to the public's view.

There had always been a sense of the impermanent and elastic in Gray's designs, and this comes to the fore in E1027 (Fig. 3). Here, the entire interior spatial organization is designed to be adaptable yet appear highly resolved at the same time. The possibility of movement is inscribed in the

15 Carmen Espegel, *Eileen Gray: Objects and Furniture Design* (Barcelona, 2013), p. 11.

16 Caroline Constant, "E. 1027: The Nonheroic Modernism of Eileen Gray," *Journal of the Society of Architectural Historians* 53 (1994): 273.

17 Shane O'Tool, "Eileen Gray: E-1027, Roquebrune Cap Martin," *archiseek*, 17 March 2002, http://archiseek.com/2002/eileen-gray-e-1027-roquebrune-cap-martin.

inbuilt furniture in the bedrooms, study, and bathrooms, and large folding screens enable a sense of privacy when closed, while also allowing open access. Articulating a distinct counter-position to Le Corbusier's dictum of the "house as machine," Gray wrote provocatively,

> The poverty of modern architecture stems from the atrophy of sensuality. ... A house is not a machine to live in. It is the shell of man, his extension, his release, his spiritual emanation. Not only its visual harmony but its entire organization, all the terms of the work, combine to render it human in the most profound sense.[18]

E1027 makes an initial impression of solidity, but closer inspection reveals that the solid is in fact a sequence of layers intersected by steps and circulation paths. The architecture critic Rowan Moore remarked that E1027 "can be considered a series of screens placed over the landscape."[19]

18 Constant, "E. 1027," 277.

19 Rowan Moore, "Eileen Gray's E1027: A Lost Legend of 20th-Century Architecture Is Resurrected," *Guardian*, 2 May 2015, http://www.theguardian.com/artanddesign/2015/may/02/eileen-gray-e1027-villa-cote-dazur-reopens-lost-legend-le-corbusier.

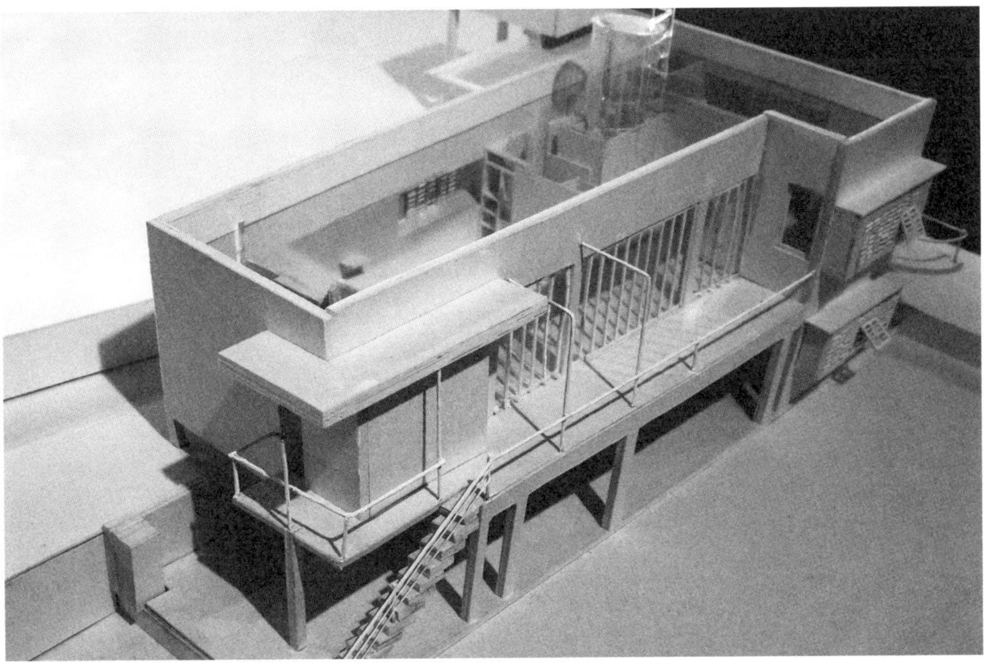

Fig. 3 Eileen Gray and Jean Badovici, *Scale model of E1027*, 1924, Photo: unknown.

Marathon Camp, Graz

Raumlaborberlin's temporary structure Marathon Camp (2012), at the Steirischer Herbst Festival in Graz, Austria, presents yet another version of nomadic space and nomadic thought in contrast to Schindler's permanent camp and Eileen Gray's le style camping (Fig. 4). The creative team around Veronika Knaup-Hasler and Florian Malzacher conceptualized a "marathon camp" to examine "artistic strategies and tactics in politics, political strategies and tactics in art."[20] For a total of 170 hours, students, artists, theorists, and activists presented critical positions on the role of art in politics and politics in art.[21] Marathon Camp was initiated as a non-hierarchical, self-organized physical and virtual open-access platform.

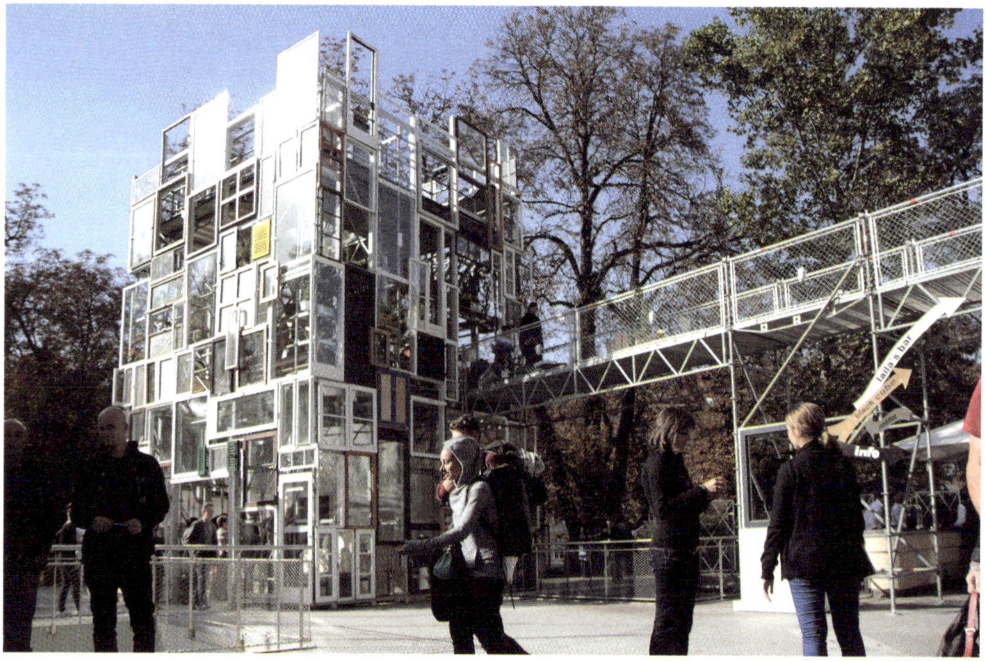

Fig. 4 Raumlaborberlin, *Marathon Camp*, Graz, 2012, Photo: unknown.

The event's motto, "Truth is Concrete," points to a lineage of critical thinking from Hegel to Lenin to Brecht, who during his exile in Denmark hung above his desk this Leninist quote: "One of the basic principles of dialectics is that there is no such thing as abstract truth, truth is always concrete."[22] In Hegel's *Logic*, the full citation is as follows:

> For the truth is concrete; that is whilst it gives a bond and principle of unity, it also possesses an internal source of development. Truth, then, is only possible as a universe or totality of thought; and the freedom of the whole, as well as the necessity of the several sub-divisions, which it implies, are only possible when these are discriminated and defined.[23]

20 Truth Is Concrete, http://www.truthisconcrete.org/about.

21 Marathon Camp ran 21–28 September 2012.

22 Vladimir Ilyich Lenin, "R. A Few Words on Dialectics: Two Revolutions," https://www.marxists.org/archive/lenin/works/1904/onestep/r.htm.

23 G. W. F. Hegel, *Hegel's Logic,* trans. William Wallace (Oxford, 1975; first published, 1892), p. 24.

The totality of truth, however, as any other absolute, or synthesis in Hegel's thinking, must be achieved through the process of dialectics in the *Aufhebung* (overcoming) of the negative, a method that finds its applied corollary in Florian Malzacher's description of Marathon Camp as a "knowledge machine" and a "communication facility" in his opening speech. Malzacher explained,

> The marathon is the center, surrounded by a camp-like living and working environment, a social space with its own needs and timings. "Truth Is Concrete" creates a one-week community, mixing day and night, developing its own jet lag towards the outside world—at the same time being open and free for everybody to join.[24]

24 Truth Is Concrete, http://www.truthisconcrete.org/about.

The "camp-like living and working environment" housing and enabling the functioning of the knowledge machine was designed by raumlaborberlin, a collective of architects based in the German capital. The collective's current nine members work both independently of each other and in varied group combinations, depending on the respective project. Common to their approach is the conviction that the contemporary urban condition is especially complex, having been solidified through convention and capital. Much of their work deals with the "upsetting" of conventional structures of both residential and commercial inhabitation and the relationship between individual and communal spatial practices through the production and insertion of temporary architectural elements and structures into the urban fabric.

The collective's work is often playful in character, as demonstrated by the Generator//Sedia Veneziana, a project for *People Meet in Architecture,* the 2010 Venice Biennale, directed by Kazuo Sejima. In Venice, raumlabor tested a modular construction system, inviting biennale visitors to build 1:1 prototypes of a new chair with the help of construction plans and manuals. The builder-visitors could then take their "Venetian chair" wherever they wanted. Stackable, the chair could, and did, on the large grounds of the biennale's *giardini* ultimately become an element within a larger sculptural construction. The chair module could also be transformed to build a table or a shelf, or a wall or a shelter, through the visitor-builder's experimentation and become an entirely self-organized or accidental spatial event or installation.

Such openness is the result of what we call space-making strategies, which collectives like raumlaborberlin and Rimini Protokoll, a theatre collective, use in creating performative and co-authored spaces as temporary alternate schemes to the fixity of the urban environment.[25] The task of designing the festival architecture for the 24/7 discursive format

25 See Thea Brejzek, "Experts of the Every-Space: Critical Space-making Strategies in Cargo Sofia-X / Cargo Asia and Ciudades Paralelas/Parallel Cities," in *Rimini Protokoll Close-Up: Lektüren,* ed. J. Birgfeld, U. Garde, and M. Mumford (Hannover, 2015), pp. 58–71.

of Marathon Camp demanded a rethinking of traditional spaces for the production and dissemination of knowledge (Fig. 5). Not unsurprisingly, the built result is much more than a pragmatic response to the brief—How to turn the festival's two main sites, the Thalia and the Opernring 7, into one interrelated environment that could both house and foster communication and discussion among a large number of festival participants, and at the same time make a statement about contemporary and alternative knowledge production?

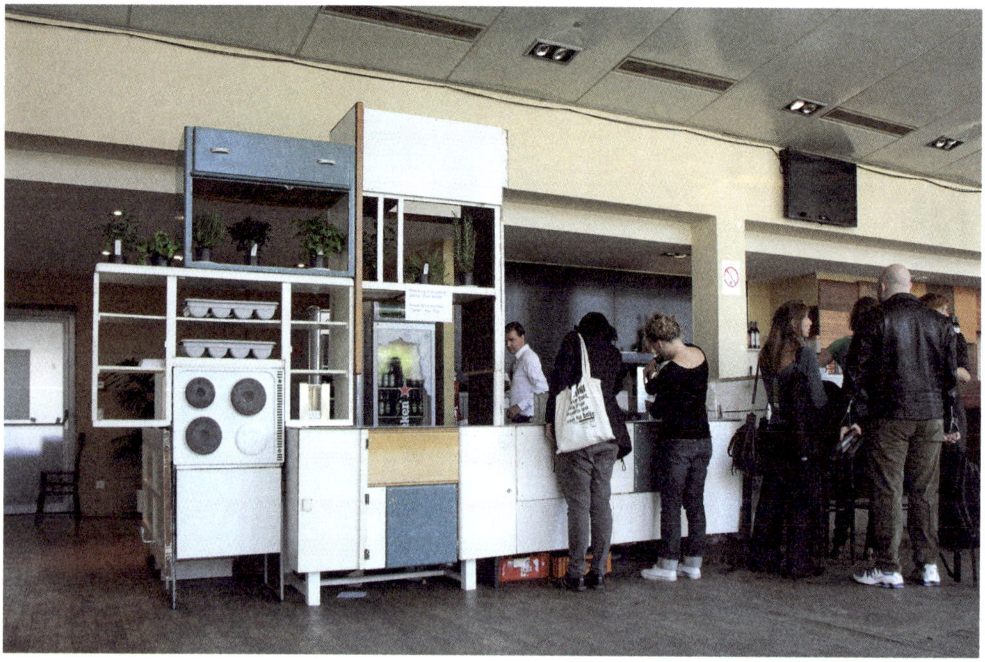

Fig. 5 Raumlaborberlin, *Marathon Camp*, Graz, interior view, 2012, Photo: unknown.

Faced with a tight budget, raumlaborberlin constructed a temporary multi-functional structure of scaffolded stairs and a bridge connecting the two main festival buildings. In addition, a multi-storey Taitlin's Tower–like construction was entirely made from recycled windows, emphasizing the improvisational nature of the event and at the same time, metaphorically, the festival's programmatic transparency of knowledge production and its conditions. The overall result was an unfinished and expandable architectural "generator" for ideas that echoes Deleuze's description of nomadology: "We seek a kind of war-machine that will not re-create a state apparatus, a nomadic unit related to the outside that will not revive an internal despotic unity."[26]

26 Deleuze, "Nomad Thought," 149.

The temporary staircase and bridge sit uncomfortably between the two main festival venues and are meant to connect and to productively interrupt ease of passage—and thought. Its continual spatial reorganization during the festival is understood as a production of scars that testifies to the visitor's active participation. The design task of situating knowledge and housing for "nomadic" thinking without borders brings to the fore the notion of the temporary and unstable. The design of a seemingly unstable structure like Marathon Camp's tower of windows sets in motion a dialectic process of positing the temporary against the fixed and the ephemeral against the constant, connecting to Hegel's dictum of the truth as concrete experience. In this way, material reality and immaterial knowledge production can create Deleuze's "informal city," where smooth spaces can be found.[27]

27 Gilles Deleuze and Felix Guattari, *A Thousand Plateaus: Capitalism and Schizophrenia*, trans. Brian Massumi (Minneapolis, 1987), p. 481.

Conclusion

The two key examples of a seemingly paradoxical phenomenon explored above are, namely, that of a modernist architecture that is "unstable" and how the origins of such design choices find an echo in Deleuze's thinking about nomadic space. The open, yet consoling space of the campfire and the basic shelter that the tent offers to the camper have been found to be equally evocative to these alternate modernist visions as the desire to embed a certain spirituality (Schindler and Gray) and social theory (Schindler) into a building's interior.

The close readings of the Kings Road House, E1027, and Marathon Camp show that Baudelaire's notion of the "fleeting and transient" next to the essential and permanent in the practices of modernity continues to have social, cultural, and political relevance. Whether articulations of the transient occur in the reinvention of domesticity toward communal living, as in Schindler's house, or in the insertion of subjectivity and intimacy into a modernist interior, as in Gray's E1027, or whether the provocative anti-aesthetics of the activist camp suggests how an informal city can develop, all of these built structures reach back to such nomadic traditions as the tent, and they are able to create and operate within a smooth space. Movements across space define the life of the nomad, who has chosen a life outside the state and its striated, hierarchical spaces. Nomadic spaces are smooth spaces that allow for free movement, Deleuze wrote. The objects discussed here do exactly that in the built environment: They allow for free movement and oscillate intriguingly between the dichotomies of stability and instability, permanence and impermanence, and all fluid and shifting states in between these binary and questionable orders of genre classification.

V

Contributors Exhibition and symposium

BELLEMO & CAT, an artist architect partnership, creates public art and architecture that is design focused and climate sensitive at the same time. They have received broad international and local recognition for projects that are adventurous and site responsive and speak globally from a local understanding. Whether the construction of a house or the twisting of a sculpture, the work of Bellemo & Cat is a wandering line of inquiry that enables them to carry the methods and results of experimentation in the fields of architecture and sculpture back and forth, like busy ants, resulting in sculptural architectural work and pragmatic approaches to urban design.

VLADIMIR BELOGOLOVSKY is the founder of the New York–based Intercontinental Curatorial Project, which focuses on organizing, curating, and designing architectural exhibitions worldwide. He is the American correspondent for the Russian architectural journal *Speech* and a corresponding member of the International Academy of Architecture in Moscow. His books include *Conversations with Architects in the Age of Celebrity* (2015), *Harry Seidler: Lifework* (2014), *Felix Novikov* (2009, 2013), *Soviet Modernism, 1955–1985* (2010), and *Green House* (2009). Belogolovsky curated the exhibition *Harry Seidler: Painting toward Architecture* at the Museum of Sydney, Australia (2014–2015), as part of his ongoing world tour Harry *Seidler: Architecture, Art and Collaborative Design* (since 2012). He graduated from the Cooper Union School of Architecture in 1996.

THEA BREJZEK, a German-born theatre scholar, is also an internationally recognized expert in scenography in and beyond the context of theatre and performance design. She is currently a professor for spatial theory at the University of Technology, Sydney, where her research involves constructions of performativity in spaces of social, cultural, and political engagement, including urban and public space, exhibitions, and media space.

AMANDA COLE is a composer of microtonal instrumental and electronic new music. She has been commissioned by, has performed at, and been recorded by Kroumata (Sweden, 2009), the ISCM Festival (New York, 2010), Ensemble Offspring (Sydney Opera House, 2011), Synergy Percussion (Casula Powerhouse, 2012), and MCA (Sydney, 2013). She was a finalist for the 2010 Blake Prize for Twitter Hymn Book and was recently awarded an Australia Council Creative Arts Fellowship.

COTTAGE INDUSTRIES is a collaboration of CRISTINA GARDUÑO FREEMAN, ANTONIA FREDMAN, and VICKI LEIBOWITZ. Their creative and theoretical projects explore intersections between architecture, design, heritage, and art through critical spatial practice and forms of participatory culture. Past projects include *The Lost Street,* a site-specific work for Expanded Architecture in The Rocks, held as part of the 2013 Sydney Architecture Festival and *Towards a New Sandwich,* a video guide to remaking a modernist icon.

KAREN CUMMINGS is the inaugural recipient of the Bushman Scholarship at the University of Newcastle for studies in voice. Since 2009 she has performed in and been a vocal coach for *Pecan Summer,* Australia's first indigenous opera. Cummings has regularly curated and broadcast programmes for the Australian Broadcasting Corporation. She has premiered new Australian works, including *Shadows and Dreams* (Whitlam Institute, University of Western Sydney), *Tales of Love* (Festival of Sydney), *Laquiem* (Studio, Sydney Opera House), and *The Audience and Other Psychopaths,* with Nigel Kellaway and Stephen Adams, and the *Opera Project* (Performance Space).

CAMPBELL DRAKE, an architect, artist, and academic, seeks to challenge conventional definitions of architecture through ideas-led practice and research. He is a lecturer in interior and spatial design at the University of Technology, Sydney, and is undertaking a PhD at RMIT University, exploring socio-architectural spatial dynamics and architectural performativity. Often working with buildings of historical and cultural significance, his recent investigative projects include the *Princess Theatre Inversion* (2014) and *Contemporary Site Investigations: Flinders Street Station* (2012).

ELIZABETH DRAKE is actively involved in composing and performing music for theatre and film as well as live performance. She is interested in the theatrical performance of music, new music, and interdisciplinary performance. Elizabeth has won numerous awards for composition and performance, including the Australian Film Institute Award for Best Original Music Score for a Feature Film, the Film Critics Circle Award for Best Music Score, and the APRA-AGSC Award for Best Feature Film Score. In 2012 she won the Green Room Award for theatre composition. Her recent live performances include Steve Reichs *Piano Phase* at the Princess Theatre (2014) and *Canto Ostinato* at WOMADelaide and at the Flinders Street Station ballroom (2012).

KATE DUNN is a practising artist and academic lecturing at UNSW Art & Design. She is currently completing a PhD at the University of Sydney, investigating creative 3D data visualizations developed through interdisciplinary collaborations with other artists, designers, and scientists. Dunn has had more than forty exhibitions nationally and internationally.

PAOLA FAVARO is a graduate of the Faculty of Architecture, Università Iuav di Venezia, Italy, and is currently senior lecturer in architecture and urban design at the University of New South Wales, Sydney. Her research examines aspects of Australian architecture and urban design and their historical and current roles in solving design problems related to the contemporary, twenty first-century city. Her research has been published in several Australian and international conference proceedings and journals. She is currently co-writing a book, *Venice Gateway,* as part of the 2014 Venice Studio in collaboration with the Università Iuav di Venezia, and she recently contributed to the Utzon International Symposium (Sydney Opera House, 2014) and the Milan Triennale exhibition *Architecture of the World: Infrastructures, City, and Landscape in the Contemporary World* (2012).

TINA FOX is a Sydney-based artist and designer. Her work operates at the intersection between art, architecture, craft, and design to challenge preconceptions about the built environment, public art, and domestic craft. By using painstaking, low-technology skills, such as crochet, she creates sculptures, installations, and environments that challenge architectural tradition and gender cliches to restore playfulness, poetics, and fragility. Her background as a trained architect has a major influence on her art practice.

RYUICHI FUJIMURA is an independent dance artist based in Sydney. He has studied contemporary dance technique as well as improvisation and choreography in Sydney and overseas. He has collaborated with both emerging and established international and Australian dance, theatre, and visual artists in various dance, theatre, opera, and site-specific performances and film projects.

PHIL GOUGH is a designer, digital artist, and PhD candidate at the University of Sydney. While researching information visualization for the non-expert user, he also teaches courses in design thinking, video production, human-computer interaction, information visualization, and creative coding at the University of Sydney and University of Technology, Sydney.

BILLY GRUNER is a practising contemporary artist and curator. He has completed a PhD in critical theory at Sydney College of the Arts, Sydney University. Gruner is the founder of MOP and SNO Contemporary Art Programmes in Sydney and is the founder and director of Modern Art Projects in the Blue Mountains, Australia.

EDUARDO KAIRUZ is an architect and artist based in Melbourne. His intentionally diffuse practice investigates notions of crisis, conflict, and dislocation found in the built and visual environments. He has published and exhibited internationally, including articles for *AD Post-Traumatic Urbanism* (2010) and *Trans/In Ordnung* (2012). His recent group exhibitions include the Prague Quadrennial (2011) and the Gwangju Design Biennale (2011). He holds a master of fine arts from Sydney College of the Arts/University of Sydney and is a PhD candidate at RMIT University. He is currently a lecturer at Monash Art Design and Architecture, where he teaches design studio and coordinates the Architecture Foundation programme.

FRANCIS KENNA is a visual artist working primarily with installation and light-based media. His practice is an ongoing investigation of perception and our engagement with the world around us. His work centres on our temporal and often tactile relationship to space, objects, and perceptual phenomena. Kenna is currently undertaking a PhD at Australian National University, Canberra, supported by an Australian Postgraduate Award.

AINSLIE MURRAY is an interdisciplinary artist, architect, and academic working principally in installation. Her work explores the augmentation of architectural space through subtle realizations of intangible, hidden, and forgotten spatial forces. The air of architectural space, the choreography of the body, and the repetitious rituals of the construction process each find a focus in Murray's work. The two- and three-dimensional works may be considered as active architectural spaces, where undulating surfaces draw attention to both artefact and process and evidence sequences of conception, assembly, and inhabitation.

KATE SHERMAN is an interdisciplinary performer and performance maker with an investigative improvisation practice. She places the body at the centre of her inquiry, and her work is visceral, physical, and imagistic. She and Ryuichi Fujimura were commissioned in 2013 to create a site-specific performance work by Performance Space for the event *30 Ways with Time and Space*. Their work, *Under Harry's Circumstances,* involved thirty performances over three evenings in thirty different locations throughout Carriageworks, Sydney. Sherman is a recipient of a Marten Bequest Travelling Scholarship and holds a bachelor of acting from the National Institute of Dramatic Art.

ELENA TORY-HENDERSON is a Sydney-based emerging artist currently completing a bachelor of fine arts with honours at the National Art School. Her practice focuses on site-specific installation. She has exhibited in numerous group shows at Studio W, the Saatchi & Saatchi Sydney office, and the National Art School. In 2014 she received the Austria Hospiz Residency Award and was selected for the John Olsen Drawing Prize.

NINA TORY-HENDERSON graduated with a bachelor of design in architecture from the University of Sydney in 2013. She is interested in the interdisciplinary potential of architecture and how it can create new ideas and methods for future practice. She was recently awarded the MADE Scholarship for multidisciplinary design and currently works at Aileen Sage Architects, a small collaborative practice.

LAWRENCE WALLEN is professor and head of the School of Design at the University of Technology, Sydney. A trained visual artist and architect, his research and practice concerns the mapping of urban spaces in such a way that their complexity and shifting nature are made visible.

LINDSAY WEBB is an architect and media artist with a special interest in aural phenomena in the built environment. His latest interdisciplinary collaborative work is *Cathode Ray Trio* (2014) for analogue electrical voltage and dancer.

Curators of the exhibition and convenors of the symposium

SARAH BREEN LOVETT is an artist, curator, PhD candidate, and academic at the University of Sydney and the University of Technology, Sydney. The working title of her PhD dissertation is "Expanded Architectural Awareness: Through the Intersection of Expanded Cinema and Architecture." Her art installations and moving images have been exhibited in Brisbane, the Blue Mountains, Kandos, Melbourne, Sydney, as well as Berlin, Dublin, London, and Rome in galleries, public art installations, and film festivals. She is the founder of Expanded Architecture, co-curator of the Cinecity Architectural Film Project, and co-curator of Modern Art Projects. She has bachelor of design, bachelor of arts, and master of architecture degrees.

CLAUDIA PERREN is an architect, curator, and academic. Since August 2014, she has served as director and chief executive officer of the Bauhaus Dessau Foundation. Previously she lectured at the University of Sydney's Faculty of Architecture, Design and Planning on curatorial practice, design, and the history and theory of architecture. Her area of interest centres primarily on the intersection of art, design, and architecture. The results of her research, teaching, and practice have been published and exhibited in Australia, the Czech Republic, Estonia, Finland, Germany, Japan, The Netherlands, Poland, Singapore, Spain, and Switzerland.

Curatorial assistants

MATTHEW ASIMAKIS
MARK BISHOP
MEILUN GAO
SHERVIN JIVANI
VICTORIA KING
SARAH LITWIN
ISABELLA MARECHAL-ROSS
GRANT MILLS
MACKENZIE NIX
BENJAMIN SPINETTI
MARK VUCKOVICH
WU YI

Acknowledgments

We would like to thank all of the institutions and individuals who supported us in the preparation of this catalogue and exhibition.

A special thank you goes to Penelope Seidler and Polly Seidler and the the academics for the peer review: Gevork Hartoonian and Suzi Attiwill; Yannis Zavoleas and Cathy Smith; Marian Macken and Christina Garduno Freeman; Nikolina Bobic and Chris Smith; Tim Ireland and Shaowen Wang.

Partners and Sponsors

Australia Square
Bauhaus Dessau Foundation
Charter Hall
DMC Creative World
Dulux
Grosvenor Place
Kawai
Leutenegger
Museum of Sydney
Seidler Architectural Foundation
Sydney Architecture Festival
Sydney Living Museums
University of Sydney

Picture Credits

COVER IMAGES: Figs. 1, 2, 3 Courtesy Harry Seidler & Associates

ENDPAPER IMAGES (PROLOG): Fig. 1.1 © Fairfax Media; Fig. 1.2 © Lend Lease Management; Figs. 1.3, 2.1, 2.2, 3.1, 3,3 © Penelope Seidler; Fig. 2.3 © Eric Sierins; Fig. 3.2 © VG Bild-Kunst, Bonn 2016 for Lin Utzon, Photo: © Penelope Seidler

ENDPAPER IMAGES (EPILOG): Fig. 1.4 © 2016 Calder Foundation, New York / Artists Rights Society (ARS), New York, for Alexander Calder, Photo: © Penelope Seidler; Figs. 1.5, 2.4, 2.5, 3.4, 3.5 © Penelope Seidler

INTRODUCTION, PP. 17–19: Fig. 1 © VG Bild-Kunst, Bonn 2016 for Max Dupain, Photo: Courtesy National Library of Australia (original negative held at The State Library of New South Wales)

BUILDINGS THAT EXPAND ARCHITECTURE, PP. 28–39: Fig. 1, © 2016 Calder Foundation, New York / Artists Rights Society (ARS), New York, for Alexander Calder, Photo: © Penelope Seidler; Fig. 2 © FLC/VG Bild-Kunst, Bonn 2016 for Le Corbusier, Photo: © Penelope Seidler; Fig. 3 © VG Bild-Kunst, Bonn 2016 for Sol LeWitt; Fig. 4 © FLC/VG Bild-Kunst, Bonn 2016 for Le Corbusier, VG Bild-Kunst, Bonn 2016 for John Olsen, Photo: © Penelope Seidler; Figs. 5, 7, 10, 13, © Penelope Seidler; Figs. 6, 12 Courtesy Harry Seidler & Associates; Figs. 8, 9 © VG Bild-Kunst, Bonn 2016 for Frank Stella; Fig. 11 © VG Bild-Kunst, Bonn 2016 for Frank Stella, Photo: © Penelope Seidler; Fig. 14 © VG Bild Kunst, Bonn 2016 for Lin Utzon, Photo: © Penelope Seidler

HARRY SEIDLER AND REDUCTIVE ART IN AUSTRALIA, PP. 56–77: Figs. 1, 5, 8, 10, 14 © Penelope Seidler; Fig. 2 © VG Bild-Kunst, Bonn 2016 for Frank Stella, Photo: © Billy Gruner; Figs. 3, 4 © Penelope Seidler, courtesy Eric Sierins; Fig. 6 © VG Bild-Kunst, Bonn 2016 for Michael Johnson, Photo: © Penelope Seidler; Fig. 8 © VG Bild-Kunst, Bonn 2016 for Hilarie Mais, Photo: © Penelope Seidler; Fig. 9 © VG Bild-Kunst, Bonn 2016 for Robert Owen, Photo: © John Marmaras; Fig. 11 Courtesy of Sullivan Strumpf Gallery; Fig. 12 © Sydney Living Museums; Fig. 13 © VG Bild-Kunst, Bonn 2016 for Ron Robertson-Swann, Photo: © Penelope Seidler

EXPERIMENTAL PRACTICES, PP. 81–112: p. 81 © VG Bild-Kunst, Bonn 2016 for Sol LeWitt, Photo: © Alex Wisser; p. 82 © VG Bild-Kunst, Bonn 2016 for Sol LeWitt, Photo: © Ian Hobbs; pp. 83, 92, 109 Photo: © Vinchy Yi Wu; pp. 84, 97, 99, 101, 104, 105, 106, 108, 112 Photo: © Alex Wisser; p. 85 © VG Bild-Kunst, Bonn 2016 for Sol LeWitt, Photo: © Vinchy Yi Wu; pp. 88, 89, 90, 93, 107, 111 Photo: © Jung Ming; p. 94 © VG Bild-Kunst, Bonn 2016 for Lin Utzon, Photo: © Jung Ming; pp. 96, 102, 103 Photo: © Olivia Govan

UNSTABLE ARCHITECTURES, PP 125–135: Figs. 1, 2 Archive of the authors; Fig. 3 © Forge mind ArchiMedia; Figs. 4, 5 © raumlaborberlin

A R

C

H

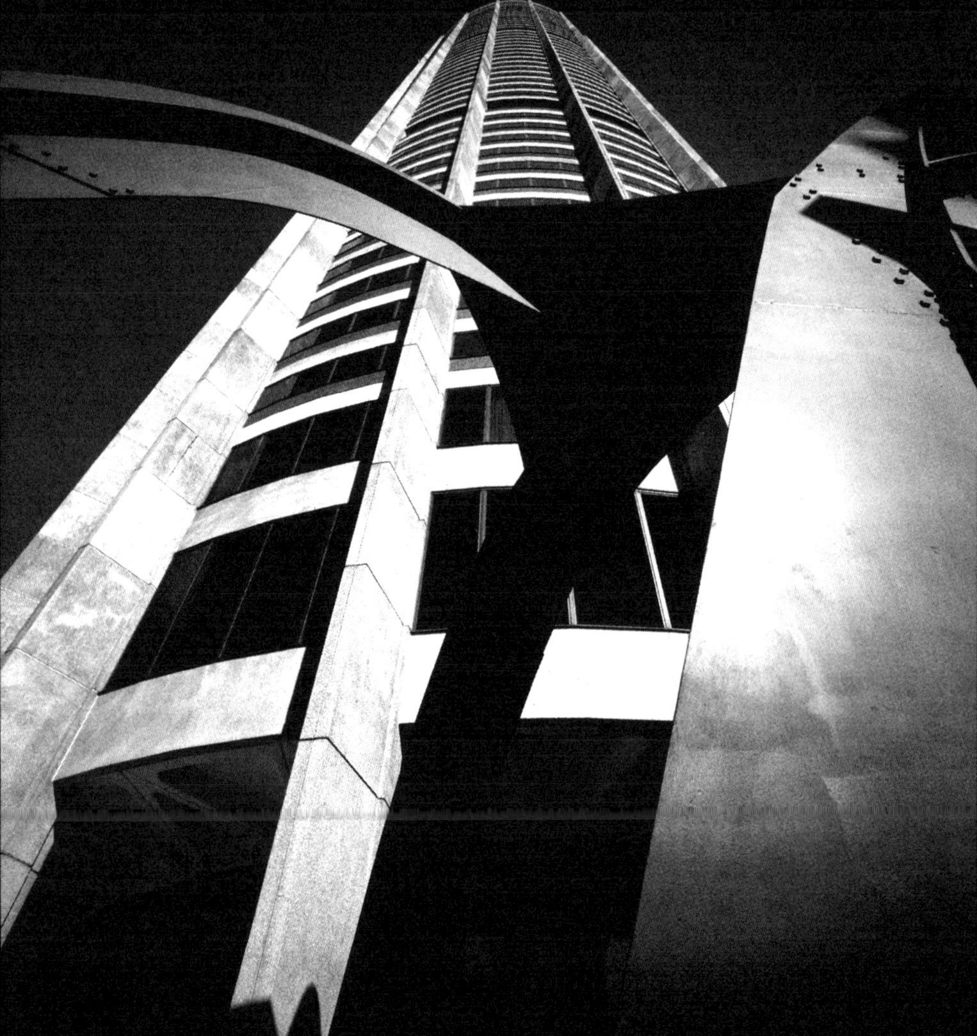

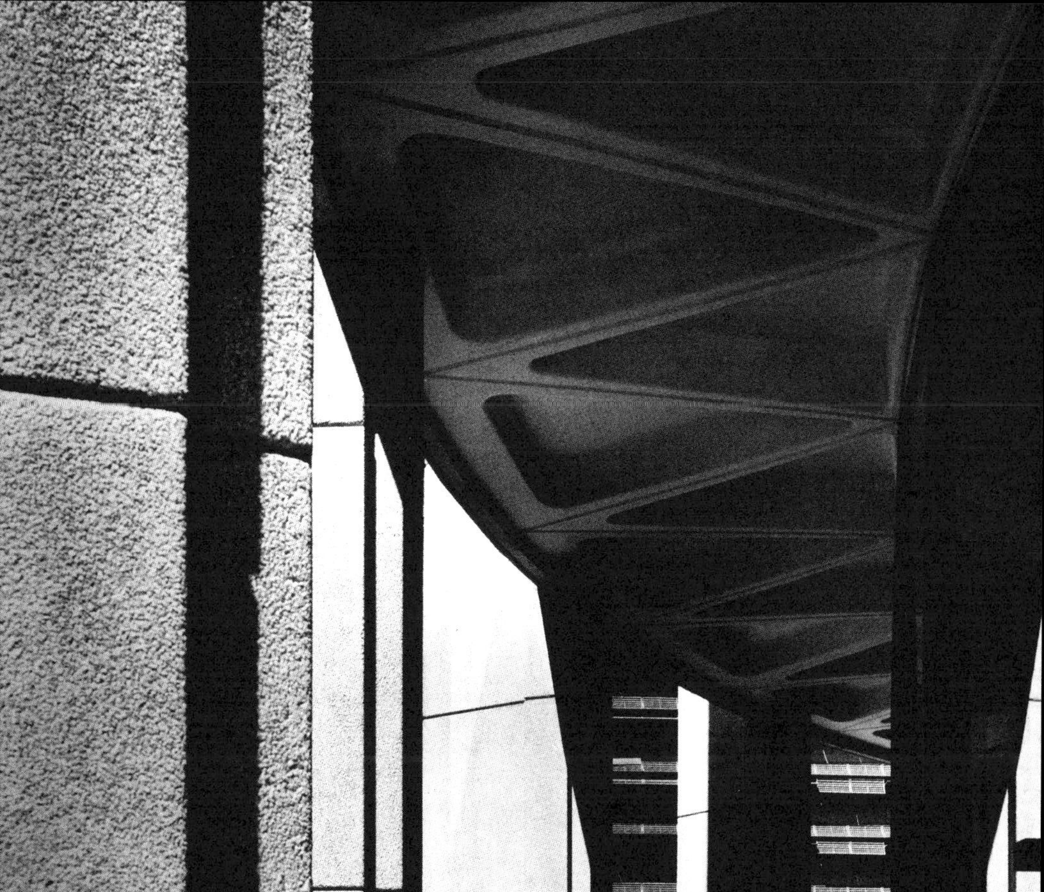

1.5

Australia Square, 1961–67.

E

C

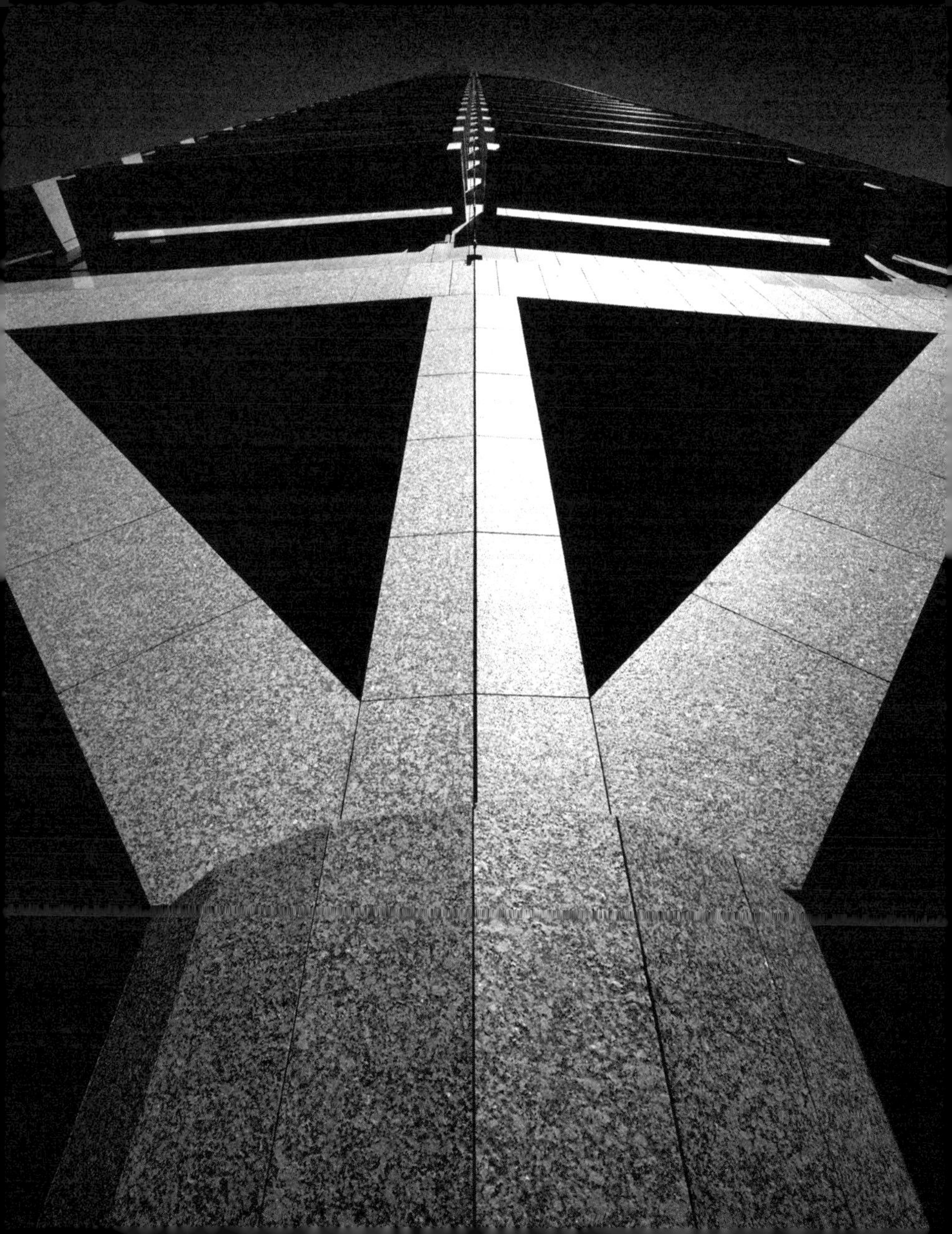

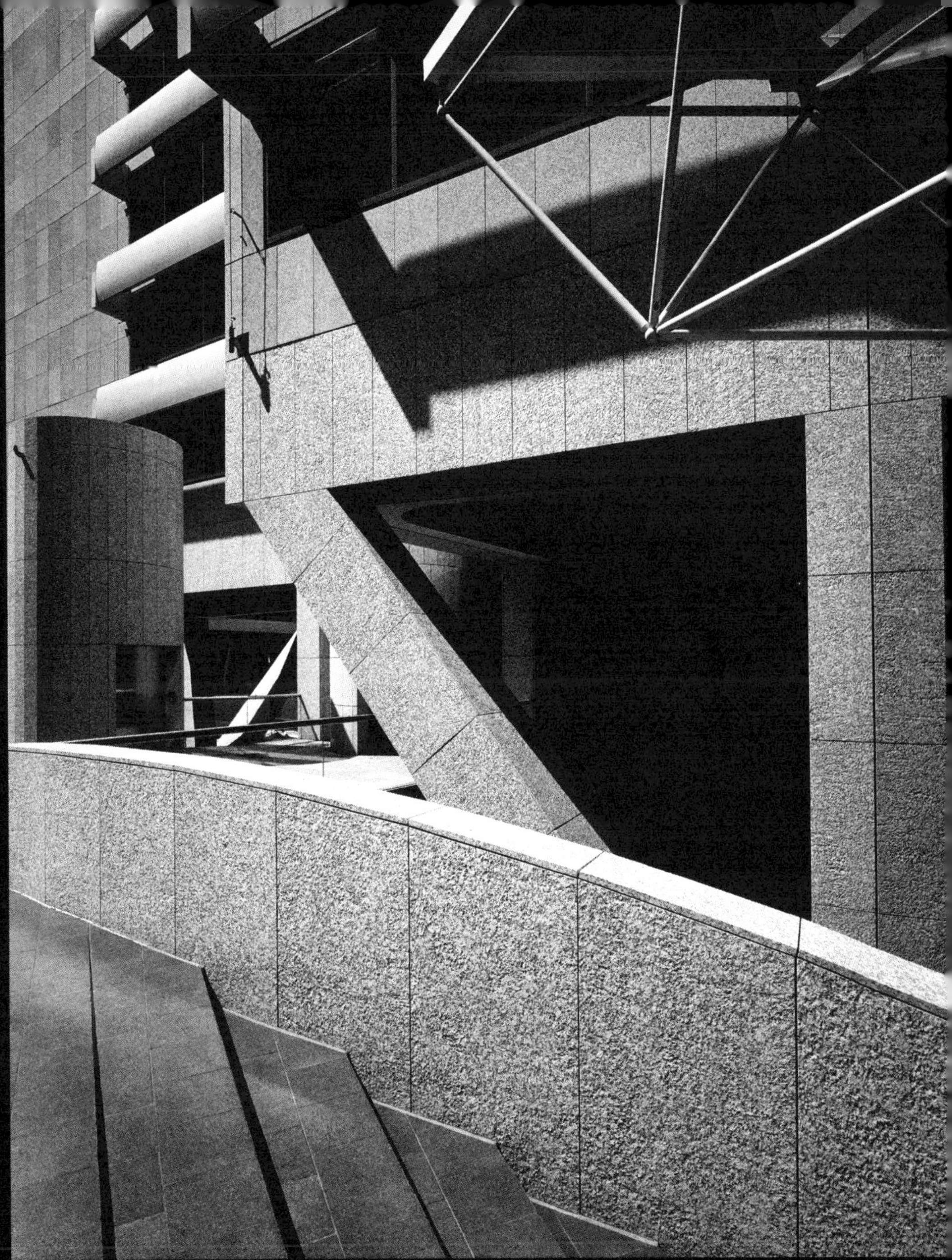

2.5

Grosvenor Place, 1982–88.

T

U

R E

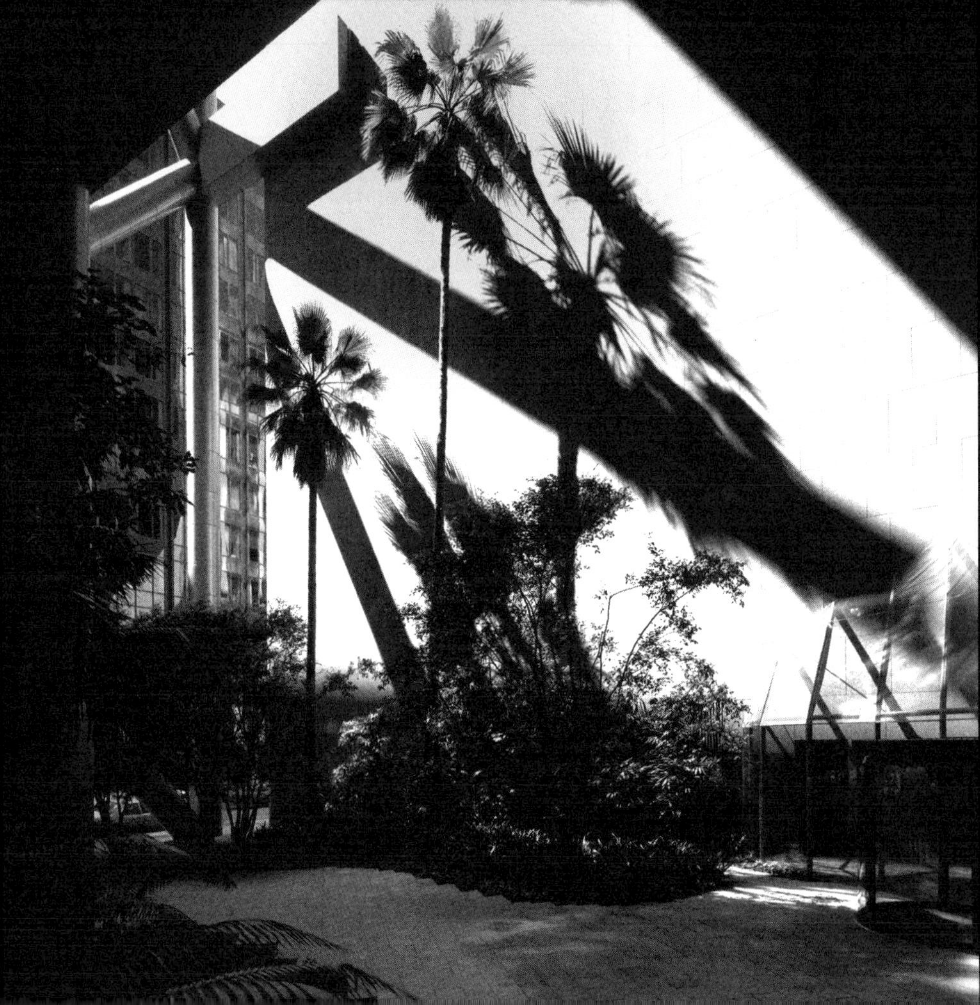

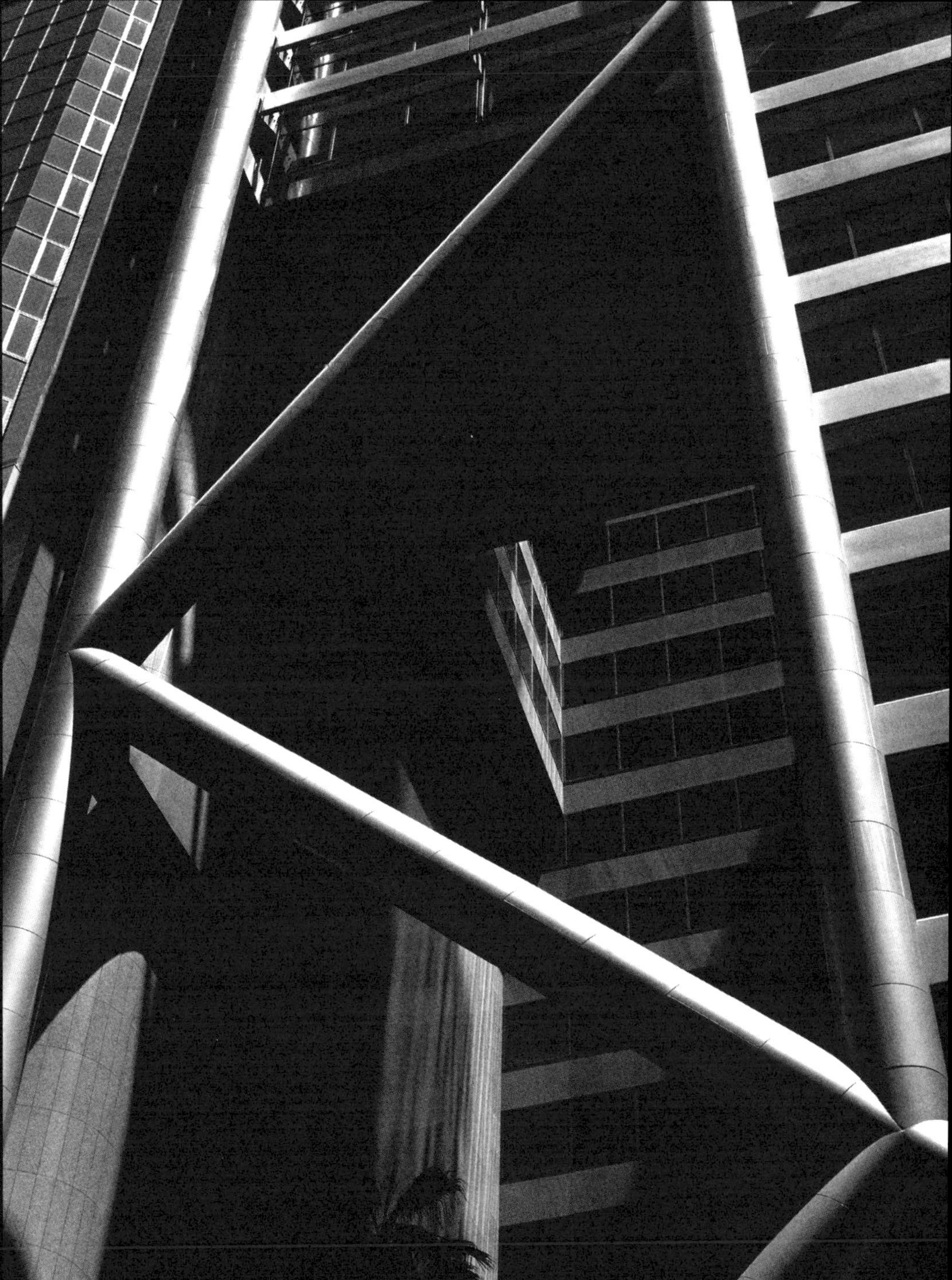

3.5

Capita Centre, 9 Castlereagh Street, 1984–89.

Imprint

This book is published in conjunction with the event and research symposium *Expanded Architecture: Temporal Formal at Seidler City*, curated by Claudia Perren and Sarah Breen Lovett, held 7–8 November 2014 at Australia Square, Grosvenor Place, Capita Centre, now 9 Castlereagh Street, and Museum of Sydney.

Editors: Claudia Perren and Sarah Breen Lovett
Managing Editor: Alexia Pooth, Bauhaus Dessau Foundation
Copyediting: Robin Surratt, Berlin
Proofreading: Katrin Globke, Bauhaus Dessau Foundation
Graphic Design: Studio Johannes Bissinger, Munich
Type setting: Johannes Bissinger, Munich / Yvonne Tenschert, Bauhaus Dessau Foundation
Typeface: Programme Regular, Italic

Bauhaus Dessau Foundation
Director Claudia Perren
Gropiusallee 38
06846 Dessau-Roßlau, Germany
www.bauhaus-dessau.de

ISBN 978-3-88778-434-8

The Deutsche Nationalbibliothek lists this publication in the Deutsche Nationalbibliografie. Detailed bibliographic data are available at http://dnb.dnb.de.

Publication © by Spurbuchverlag
1. print run 2016
Am Eichenhügel 4,
96148 Baunach, Germany

AADR—Art Architecture Design Research publishes research with an emphasis on the relationship between critical theory and creative practice.

AADR Curatorial Editor:
Rochus Urban Hinkel, Stockholm

Production: pth-mediaberatung GmbH, Würzburg

For further information on Spurbuchverlag and AADR visit www.aadr.info / w ww.spurbuch.de.